How to Deal with the Media

Dennis Barker spent most of his journalistic career on *The Guardian* after local and regional journalism in East Anglia and the Midlands. He has been a reporter, feature writer, theatre and film critic and columnist. For *The Guardian* he was media correspondent and writer of various columns, including a daily people profile of various men and women in the news. After passing the National Council for the Training of Journalists' National Proficiency Training Certificate he became one of the first journalists in Britain to gain the NCTJ's newly introduced higher, degree-standard qualification, the National Diploma in Journalism. He is also a novelist and broadcaster.

Also by Dennis Barker

Non-fiction
The Craft of the Media Interview
Soldiering On
Ruling the Waves
Guarding the Skies
One Man's Estate
Parian Ware
Fresh Start

Novels
Candidate of Promise
The Scandalisers
Winston Three Three Three

How to
Deal with the Media

A Practical Guide

DENNIS BARKER

ROBERT HALE · LONDON

ISBN 0 7090 6621 X

Robert Hale Limited
Clerkenwell House
Clerkenwell Green
London EC1R 0HT

2 4 6 8 10 9 7 5 3 1

Typeset by
Derek Doyle & Associates, Liverpool.
Printed by Gutenberg Press Limited, Malta

Contents

How to Deal with the Media

Introduction

Facing the media is torture to some people, especially the inexperienced and those with a lot to lose; what should be thought of as an opportunity is dreaded as a sore trial.

Appearing on television or national radio, in particular, can seem a threat to your personality, your job, your self-possession, your sense of being in control.

Yet in these days of increasing media presence the chances are that almost everyone – including you – will at some stage have to talk to someone from the media, be it from a national or local newspaper, a magazine, a local radio station or a television channel.

Will you handle it well or badly? You can be sure of two things.

First, if you are completely inexperienced, some under-standing of the media's needs and how their journalists operate will make things less frightening for you. Second, even if you are fairly used to meeting the media, and on the whole like it, you could – with more knowledge and perception – handle it even better.

Such knowledge and perception is what this book seeks to provide and stimulate. It is not something that can be taught systematically by rote, because every encounter with the media is different. But it should be possible for the reader to assimilate rules and hints that can be adapted to his or her own needs.

In this new millennium new technologies like digital broadcasting, the internet and email – and the successors which will make them obsolete in their turn – will alter the mechanics of the way journalists do their job. However, you need not be intimidated by technologies. Journalism and the media will continue to depend crucially on what they have always depended upon: not machinery, but human beings who are prepared to talk.

Human beings, in short, who are like you – especially if you are able to talk to the media skilfully and to your own best advantage.

For the sake of brevity and in an effort to avoid clumsy wording, I have used the term 'he' when referring to journalists or to those who deal with them, when I could equally appropriately have said 'she'.

1 The Basic Fact

Every journalist who contacts you, in whatever way, wants a story and is determined to get one. You have no control over that fact. But you do have some control over – or at least influence upon – the *sort* or story he gets.

From your point of view, news stories are of two types: the ones you want to see published, and those you would prefer not to see published. But the journalist who sees you recognizes no such distinction; he is interested only in news values. From his point of view, your dying of cancer would be as good a story as your being cured of cancer. That is an uncomfortable fact, but it is one that anyone who deals with the media has to live with.

As private individuals journalists vary as all other types of people vary. If they met you in the club or pub as a private individual, most of them would rather you were cured of cancer than died of it. But they do vary. As private individuals, some are amoral, others more scrupulous; a few are stupid, others are highly intelligent. Some are thick-skinned, others sensitive; some are careless, others careful. Some have tunnel vision, where others can see the broader picture, and while some have a rigorous awareness of reality, others have a more muddied one.

But all journalists have one thing in common: in their professional capacities they are (in descending order of merit) serving the cause of truth; serving their readers, listeners or viewers; serving their bosses; serving their own egos in relation to their competing colleagues. What they are *not* serving is *you*.

Do not attempt to deal with a journalist as you would a doctor, priest, lawyer or shop assistant, expecting unqualified personal help and understanding. That is not his function. His function is to provide a service to the reader, listener or viewer, not to you.

Even so, there could be some ways in which a journalist could write his story that would be more in your interest than other ways. And how to influence a favourable outcome rests largely with you, not with him. If you feed him facts that, while helpful to him, are incidentally to your advantage, so much the better for you. The story is more likely to be favourable to you than if you antagonize him by reticence or evasiveness.

One of the most irritating things that can happen to a journalist is for a contact not to bother to feed him the full information, and then to claim that his report is inaccurate or inadequate. At the most rudimentary level this can occur when, for example, a junior reporter in a county town is sent to cover a local gymkhana.

Almost a stranger to the razor, and knowing little about horses in general or gymkhanas in particular, the young reporter arrives at the field where the event is taking place and looks around for someone to talk to. No one recognizes him or comes forward to help. He asks someone who is in charge of the event, and is told it is the president of the Bodcaster Light Horse Club, Sir Justin Somethingorother, who will probably be found in the visitors' hospitality tent.

Sir Justin, who has a large whisky and soda in his hand and is talking to the Lord Lieutenant, is 'far too busy' to talk to the young reporter or to refer him to someone else who will deal with him. A trifle alienated, and therefore not at his best, the reporter nevertheless stops the rider who has just won a race and asks him his name, and goes on doing this for every winner during the afternoon. Some of the winners, however, appear to be 'too busy' to answer his questions.

After his report appears Sir Justin (now apparently not too busy to write letters to newspaper editors) complains that not all of the winners have been listed, some of their names have been mis-spelt, and in particular the reporter has missed the fact that the rider who won one event in 2 minutes 39 seconds broke a record that had stood since 1946, when the gymkhanas were re-established after the war ended. This, says Sir Justin, is thoroughly symptomatic of the fall in standards in the media.

Was he right? He was not.

It is true that the onus is always on the journalist to make sure that his facts are complete and accurate – that, technically, is his responsibility, whether he is a beginner on the *Bodcaster Weekly Bugle* or an experienced journalist on *The Times* or *The Guardian*. In practice, though, there is little point in blaming a journalist afterwards for not getting the correct and full facts. It is more useful to blame yourself for not helping him to get them.

Arrangements for press coverage at the gymkhana should have been made in advance. Far from puffing himself up as too important to talk to a fresh-faced young reporter from 'the local rag', Sir Justin should have temporarily interrupted his conversation with the Lord Lieutenant, greeted the reporter as if he was a valued guest, told him, 'We've fixed you up with the secretary/press secretary/other officer to look after you and make sure you get all you want', and either introduced the journalist to that person or else pointed him out so that the reporter could introduce himself.

The designated person would have known exactly how to spell the names of all the contestants, would have volunteered a few interesting facts about the past performances of each, and certainly would have pointed out to the reporter that at one point a 1946 record had been broken.

Do not fail to take trouble over briefing a journalist and then complain afterwards that, in effect, he was unbriefed.

Of course, the higher the stakes get, right up to governmental level, the more difficult the decision about briefing gets, but the principle remains the same. In a democracy adverse points of view are not difficult to obtain if a government spokesman tries to avoid discussing any subject. It will almost always be better to offer something than to offer nothing at all. Nothing inflames a journalist more certainly than an empty notebook. Conversely, nothing soothes a journalist more than a full one – perhaps even to the point when he will not bother to question other people who may be expected to have an axe to grind.

At the very top, statecraft may sometimes involve lying or economy with the truth; but, even here, the closer a briefing is kept to the truth the better. If a journalist asks a Prime Minister whether he intends to invade a neighbouring country, and the Prime Minister replies, 'No', then, when the following week the troops start to advance, the Prime Minister's credibility will have been seriously damaged. It would have been far more politic for the Prime Minister to have rehearsed with the media the possibilities open to him (in this way, theorizing can be made to appear to be a sharing of confidences) without saying what he would or wouldn't in fact do.

In practice, Prime Ministers or other government ministers may not need such advice: most are already well, or at least copiously, served by spin doctors. But the fact remains that maximum apparent frankness is one of the most efficient methods of deception. You cannot necessarily prevent unpalatable facts from ultimately reaching the media, but you may, for a useful period of time, crowd them out by ensuring that media notebooks and clipboards are full of your own facts and opinions.

At whatever level, over-briefing is usually a less perilous path than under-briefing or complete evasion. The point will be dealt with in more detail later.

The foregoing assumes that you have facts which, ideally, you would like to hide. But what if, on the contrary, you have facts which you wish to bring out – perhaps about a new product your employers have made, or about an achievement of your own? Here again, you cannot dictate what the journalist will write, or even be sure that he will write anything at all. But there are ways to influence the final result so that it is likely to be more satisfactory to you. This point, too, will be dealt with in more detail later.

In essence the results will be better the more you understand the journalist's professional needs, his personal identity and the constraints against which he has to work. Only then will you have a more confident hope of making media exchanges more beneficial from your point of view – and that confidence itself will become one of the ingredients of success in dealing with the media.

2   Suddenly of Interest

Many people who face journalists for the first time, simply because they happen to have become relevant to the news, make the same mistake that less educated laymen tend to make when required to 'write' something. Imagining that their usual way of expressing themselves won't do, and that they must now start writing or talking a language called 'Writer-ese' or 'Media-ese', they assume that only a sort of affected imitation of their usual way of expressing themselves will meet the case. They are heading up a blind alley, and a potentially embarrassing one.

Facing journalists does not require the use of a new 'language' different from the one you normally use (though you may need to refine it somewhat, purging it of some of the 'ers' and 'ums' and 'you knows' and sundry expletives). You should not be false to yourself. On the contrary, when faced with a journalist be as natural as possible. *You* are in control – in so far as anyone, anywhere, is ever really in control of events. You don't want to talk to him, he wants to talk to *you*. That gives you an advantage from the start. In ninety-nine cases out of a hundred, the questions addressed to media-inexperienced people are merely searches for information, rather than traps. Even so, if you don't want to answer questions, no journalist can force you to. And, if you do answer and are badly misrepresented, there are bodies to whom you can complain.

If you have seen a bad road crash you may have no time to prepare your answers to questions from journalists. In practice, though, you need only ask yourself briefly what exactly you have seen, give yourself the answer as concisely as possible, and then repeat that answer to the journalist.

If you feel that the accident illustrates a point that needs to be made in the public interest (for example that there should be clear danger signs along the stretch of road where the accident happened), think about precisely what that point is, and express it as shortly and with as few histrionics as you can. 'There have been a lot of accidents near where this accident happened and there ought to be clear danger signs there' is all you need say.

But if you go on with the argument and suddenly lose the thread, admit that fact at once and go back to the beginning of the thought you were following when your mind blanked out. In such circumstances, it is not in the journalist's interest to make you look stupid, and you will almost certainly find that your fumblings, if any, will be edited out of the print, radio or television report – unless it is thought that they vividly illustrate the strain you have been under.

At national level, a large pack of journalists can seem intimidating until you remember that, if you are terrified of them, each of them as an individual is even more terrified of being beaten by his rivals in the competition for important or sensational facts or angles.

If, as a resident of some prosperous and pretty street in London with historical associations with Florence

Nightingale and Edward VII, you lead or take part in a sit-down protest against the heavy lorries that are now using it as a short cut, you may be alarmed when cameramen and reporters arrive en masse – especially as the only reason you are there is that you enjoy your peace and quiet. But what the media need is a story, and it is in your interests to give them the best one possible to put your point across. The less you think about yourself, and what sort of figure you are cutting, the better.

This applies even if television cameras are watching you. Very rarely indeed in such circumstances are television cameras used to make inexperienced people look stupid: it would excite immediate resentment among viewers, who are far more likely to empathize with you as a 'civilian' than they are with professional journalists.

Have your arguments clear in your mind before the press gang arrives, and stick to the points you have decided to make. Repeat them as often as you are required to, without betraying impatience. If some journalists arrive late, make sure you approach them to ensure that they are properly briefed from your point of view. The fact that you are inexperienced may even count as an advantage: steadfast simplicity can hold its own against sophisticated manipulation.

How do you make absolutely sure that you will come out of your first contacts with journalists unscathed? There is no way of doing this – all statements made to the media may just possibly rebound in some way that cannot be predicted. But if you know what you want to say – what you saw and heard, what your strongest arguments are, what you feel most passionately about and why – you have a good chance of coming out of your very first media encounters smelling of roses and with your reputation intact – certainly among the sort of people to whom you are trying to appeal.

One other thing may be predicted about your first contact with the media, even if it is unexpected and happens only by accident: you will learn a lot from it. You will be able to see where you did well and where you did badly. You will be able to see the mistakes you made, and this will help you if ever you have contacts with the media again.

In particular, the second time round you should aim not to let bluster get you into a fluster. Always stand your ground and say pleasantly what you want to say. If you are not a serial killer, fraudster or rapist, you should avoid behaving defensively and giving the impression that you might be.

3 Attitudes

The most unproductive, and even dangerous, mistake that can be made by someone who dreads talking to the media is to regard such an encounter as a threat rather than an opportunity. Journalists are in a sense predators, and predators are programmed to smell and exploit fear. However, unless you are peddling lies or deception you need not feel such a dread.

As the sensationalist press concerns itself more and more with sexual gossip about television actors and models, there is little chance that the average person with an average non-sensational story to tell will receive any attention at all from it, friendly or unfriendly. And quality newspapers and magazines, despite tabloidizing pressures, are still capable of treating a straightforward story in a straightforward way. Furthermore, many if not most people who spend a lot of their time talking to the media talk to specialist publications or programmes, in which it is possible to make your points without great fear of distortion or other trickery.

But, of course, any contact with the media can blow up in your face unless you pay careful attention to what you are doing. It is all very well for advisers to say, 'Be very careful but don't worry'. The advice may be sound, but it is rather like sitting in a dentist's chair, with the drill half an inch from your decayed tooth, and being told to relax – it is easier said than done. All the same, it is the best advice available: you are less likely to get hurt that way.

You will aim to relax in the sense that an actor must learn to relax when he is on stage: unless you relax, your brain will not work at its best. Its internal channels of communication will freeze, you will start to put feet wrong, perhaps badly wrong, and you will show yourself and those for whom you speak in a bad light.

Write in the steam on your bathroom mirror: 'It's an OPPORTUNITY'. Once you see and accept the reality of this statement, you can start exploiting an encounter with the media in a positive way that will itself help to drive out fear. Make yourself so familiar with the arguments you want to produce that you know that, if need be, you will be able to hold your own without notes.

That great psychiatrist Alfred Adler (now the most unfairly neglected of the great Vienna Three – Freud, Jung and Adler) said that it was impossible merely to remove fear from the mind: you could only *replace* it with something else, preferably 'fight'. The notion of replacing fear with fight is especially helpful to someone who is nervous about facing the media.

Never face the media voluntarily unless you have a definite reason for doing so. But if you have such a reason, then you must 'fight' in an aggressive (thrusting, but not belligerent) way to put your case across. Being aggressive in this context means actively wanting to put your points, rather than merely being prepared to have them drawn out of you like teeth. It means going back and completing your

answers if you are interrupted. It means using every hesitation on the interviewer's part to step in and further elab-
orate what you are saying.

In its externals, as distinct from its content, any media
encounter can be regarded as a game, if that makes you
feel better. (It is ironic that so many sportsmen fail to take
the point and lumber their way nervously through media
interviews with a clumsiness they would never display on
the football field, cricket pitch or tennis court. Being a
'celebrity', or even a celebrity, does not automatically make
you articulate.) Imagine yourself on a tennis court with the
media person on the other side of the net. You are not
frightened of that player, you do not hate that player, you
are not contemptuous of that player, *but* you watch his
every move carefully, and you fully intend to return with
relish any shot he puts across the net. That is one way
forward if you are of a nervous disposition.

But suppose that, on the contrary, you are an open,
extrovert person who finds himself talking nineteen to the
dozen in most situations. The advice here would be quite
different.

When talking to the media, say what you intend to say –
or as much of it as you can manage to say – *but no more*,
however much you may be prompted by 'friendly' questions. Friendly questions can be the most dangerous of the
lot, because they will encourage you to open up in a way
that visibly dangerous questions could never do.

Whatever the context, a good journalist will try to keep
you talking. He does this on the same principle that, in
war, an interrogator will try to keep an enemy prisoner
talking. The theory is that a person who has to keep talking will inevitably produce more information or insights

because of the simple human reluctance to keep on saying the same thing or things; it bores the questioned human being as much as it does the questioner.

The happy extrovert character should do precisely as the buttoned-up character does in at least one respect. He should rehearse in his mind the basic message he is trying to put across until he knows it inside out. He should then do the same with any background facts he is willing to discuss. If necessary (if he cannot speak silently in his own mind) he should shut himself in his bedroom, out of earshot of other human beings, and speak the answers to imagined questions.

He should also anticipate in his mind what form dangerous questions could take, and rehearse the answers he will give to them if he cannot escape answering. In the interview itself, however, he should keep as far away from the danger areas as possible – if necessary by changing the subject to an *apparently* more newsy one.

The more open and garrulous you are, the easier you will find it to exploit the positive sides of the 'opportunity' that any media meeting presents you with. On the other hand, you will find it more difficult invisibly to bite your tongue when you have said all you need to say, and when anything further could only confuse or spoil the total picture. The remedy is to learn how to shut up. This may entail a painful reappraisal of yourself in relation to the world.

Do not let your vanity persuade you that a journalist finds you fascinating as a human being: he is after a story. When you have given him a good story on, let us say, a new product you are developing, do not spoil that story by allowing some of your doubts to leak out in the final moments of the encounter. Do not too readily assume that you have not explained yourself adequately and must say something more in order to make matters more clear. If a journalist finds something unclear, he will ask you further questions; if he doesn't, you must assume that he has understood all that, from your point of view, he needs to understand.

To what extent should you allow yourself to like a journalist personally and tailor your answers to him as a person? That process can be flattering to a journalist – everyone likes to be appreciated as a human being. But, if you do this, once the journalist leaves your presence he may possibly feel he has somehow been conned, and take a sterner line with you and your material than he otherwise would have done, just to show his shrewdness and independence. There is also the danger that, in trying to tailor what you say so as to charm the journalist, you will lose the thread of your best line of argument. Keep your mind on the point or points and relegate the journalist's personality, if it is congenial, to the status of a minor but valued bonus.

In particular, do not tell a journalist far more than you need to, or than is good for you and the story you are putting over, and 'trust' him not to use the compromising parts of the interview because you have known him a long time, and he is a good chap, and you think he thinks you are a good chap. You cannot 'trust' a journalist to blind himself to what is, for him, a good story, any more than you can 'trust' your doctor to blind himself to an illness you have or a policeman to blind himself to a crime you have committed. In any of these cases, it would go against the nature of their vocation, and if they were honest practitioners of that vocation, they couldn't and wouldn't do it.

It is possible to tell journalists things 'off the record'. Presented with an opportunity to talk to a member of the media who seems friendly (and indeed may *be* friendly) it is tempting, if you want to say more than you ideally should say, to insist beforehand that it is off the record. Don't place too much reliance on this formula, though. The journalist may be pressured by his news desk or editor somehow to get round the undertaking. He may talk to other journalists, who may feel no obligation to you. He may genuinely be confused about which parts of the talk were off the record and which were on the record – especially if you repeatedly keep going on and off the record.

It is safest to assume that anything said to a journalist will one day be *on* the record – if not today, then tomorrow or the day after – whether through him and his work or through someone else and his work. Though any meeting with the media is indeed an opportunity (and should be regarded as such, rather than as a combat course), this fact should always be borne in mind. Especially if you are a natural talker, impose limits on yourself and what you say. Evolve a repertoire of responses to possible questions and stick to those, however 'friendly' the questioning.

So much for realities. What about something apparently more superficial – the personal impression, genuine or phoney, you leave on the media people to whom you talk?

If you are an out-going type, you will almost certainly find it easier to have that confidence without which you will not be able to make the best of your opportunity. You will also find it easier to radiate the *impression* of confidence. But, if you are a less outgoing type, do not assume that you will necessarily be at a disadvantage. Once you learn how to use your own personality, whatever that may be, you should be on virtually level terms with other people.

If you are a man of few words, you can even make that into an act which will raise a few laughs and perhaps save you from some difficult questions (journalists may, just may, shrink from asking them, for fear of a succinct put-down). One successful politician, faced on live television with an ingenious question no one had ventured to ask him before, and which would land him in deep trouble whether he answered 'Yes' or 'No', merely wagged his forefinger at his questioner and said, 'Naughty, naughty!' Another, facing a shouted question from the press table as he left a public meeting, said 'Stupid question!' and moved on. And a media mogul at a press conference asked a difficult question about his company's future intentions, replied 'That is a naïve question, even for you' and asked for the next question.

It is true that such terse escape routes have become less fashionable and less effective as the media have increased their power. Even so, it remains true that a succinct, introspective personality can trade on the fact of his identity just as an expansive personality can trade on his, *if* he keeps his nerve.

You are (presumably) not a criminal nor a pathological liar. Do not behave as if you are. Believe that your personality is valid. Whatever it may be, that personality is the one through which you will have to deal with the media. Maintain it whatever emotional tone the interviewer seeks to impose.

Do not allow yourself to be hounded by what the questioner wants to talk about. Use his questions to talk about what *you* want to talk about, and do it with a pleasant smile, even if you could cheerfully strangle the fellow.

All this will come much more easily if you always remember the golden rule that a media encounter is an opportunity, not a punishment: that should be your central attitude. If it is not an opportunity – if there is nothing you can achieve through undergoing it – then you should simply not make yourself available. If there is no prospective gain, it is unwise to chance a possible loss.

There is no legal obligation to talk to the media and, as far as the public memory is concerned, it will soon forget whether you made yourself available or declined to do so, just as it will forget which questions you answered and which questions you declined to answer. As for the public, it notices and remembers much less about what has gone on between the media and the people it deals with than the media itself does. Sometimes it may even enjoy seeing two fingers apparently being held up to the omnipresent media.

4 Timing

Answer media questions at a time that suits you as well as the questioner. Don't allow yourself to be bounced into saying anything at an unsuitable time. Stonewall if necessary until you are fully briefed and prepared.

Imagine that you are spokesman for the local fire service, and an MP for a different constituency suggests in the House of Commons that turn-out times in the nation's fire brigades are getting worse. Obviously this is a story that merits attention from the media, both local and national.

The way you should deal with local newspapers and radio and television journalists will probably be fairly straightforward, and you will be quite likely to know the reporter or specialist put on to the story. You say merely, 'Ben, I'm looking into this at this moment. I'll ring you back within the hour.'

You then call the chief of the local fire service and get from him the facts about turn-out times locally. If these are better than they were last year, rather than worse, you ring the journalist back and say simply, 'Ben, I've checked this out, and in our own case turn-out times have actually improved since last year'; you then give him the statistics that back this claim up.

What you do *not* do when the journalist rings is say, 'We are looking into this crisis'; that could lead to the headline 'Crisis at Fire Service'. Nor do you say, 'Oh yes, Ben, I've heard these rumours, but we've been trying to improve'. The result of that could be a headline like 'Trying to Improve!' – which suggests that your fire service is inadequate but trying not to be.

Say nothing that can be used against you until you have checked out the facts. Don't be rushed. It is better to say, 'I can't say anything yet, but when exactly is your deadline?' This indicates that you know something about how reporters have to work and are willing to take that into consideration, but are not going to be stampeded into saying anything off the cuff. If the reporter has to say that his deadline is not until five in the afternoon, he is not morally in a position to start pushing you into making some sort of statement at twelve noon.

Suppose the local fire service does indeed have worse turn-out times than it had last year? Not so easy! In this case you will eventually have to acknowledge the downturn without attempting to fudge the issue, but you are entitled, before finally speaking to the reporter, to amass some facts that will put your fire service's performance in a more favourable light.

It will pay you, in such a case, to contact a number of counterparts in other parts of the country and ask them what their own fire services' turn-out times have been like. (You can do this under the general heading of pooling information – you can let them know your own figures.) Then when you speak to the reporter, you may be in a position to say, 'Ben, it is true that our turn-out times have not been as good as last year's, but in comparison with other areas in the country it seems we have done better than most.' The aim should not be to shuffle off responsibility for your own fire service's performance, but to be able to quote some facts that will put the situation in a better light.

How should you deal with national newspapers, radio and television in the same sort of situation? Suppose you are the same local spokesman, but this time it is a national newspaper reporter who rings you up. He says, 'We are doing a story on the turn-out times of fire services following today's mention in the House of Commons. We are ringing a number of local services for spot-checks. What is the situation in your area?' You reply 'I am looking into the situation at the moment and will ring you back'. But this time the reporter says, 'Are you saying you don't know the position in your own fire service? Other areas we have telephoned have answered the question.'

What you do *not* say to this is, 'To the best of my memory our turn-out figures have actually improved.' Why don't you say this? Because you may be wrong. If you are, the reporter is entitled to write, 'Boxborough fire service at first suggested that it had improved its performance but later had to admit that its average turn-out time was worse than it was last year by one minute fifty seconds.' This suggests that you have been shifty and have been found out.

Neither do you rise to the bait of 'but everyone else has answered the question'. Perhaps they have, perhaps they haven't; it is not unusual for reporters who want to get a story in a hurry (a perfectly natural ambition in a journalist) to use the 'everyone else has' argument. It should be resisted. The time to talk to the media is when you are in possession of the central fact and surrounding facts.

Providing you don't overrun a reporter's deadline, you can afford to remain silent.

Any remark you may make before you are briefed may be twisted against you. If you say 'I don't know what the turn-out times are' you can be represented as someone who is too ill-informed to do his job efficiently. If you say 'I have been asked not to say anything at the present stage', you will almost certainly face the supplementary question, 'Who is trying to prevent you talking? The leader of the council's ruling political party?' If you are unbriefed, the less said the better. 'I'll ring you back' is the safest thing to say – provided you make sure you *do* ring back in time.

Delaying until after the journalist's deadline in the hope of killing the story is, from your own point of view, a high-risk procedure. You will antagonize the journalist concerned, who will be convinced – and tell his colleagues – that you are either devious or incompetent.

Except in exceptional circumstances, undertakings to ring back should be honoured. If near his deadline a journalist has to ring *you* back, and finds he can't get through because so many other journalists are wanting to talk to you, he will be intensely irritated and not disposed to treat you kindly. Moreover, he may well write the dreaded sentence: 'A spokesman for Boxbridge fire service said, "I will ring back," but did not do so.'

Always ring back. Always respond. But respond at a time when you are best equipped to deal with the issue, not necessarily when the journalist would ideally (from his point of view) like you to talk. All journalists would like a story five minutes ago, but it will be in your best interests not to be bounced by this pressure into making half-cock statements or remarks. Do not in any circumstances be lured into going against your own instinct and judgement.

Respond to the objective fact of deadlines, rather than to psychological pressure.

5   Anticipate

If a question ever catches you off guard, it is by definition your own fault: you have not anticipated and prepared thoroughly enough. If a questioner can prepare a question that is difficult to answer, you can prepare an answer that is difficult to fault – unless your position is *completely* untenable, in which case unvarnished honesty in the hope of gaining sympathy may be the best (or only) available policy.

Suppose that you are a footballer whose recent performances on the field have been far from your best. There have been a number of recent stories suggesting that various named footballers, including you, have been questioned by their club officials about the taking of bribes from gambling interests for helping to lose matches by playing badly.

You have not been taking bribes of any sort. So surely all you have to do is to say that you have simply been off form recently, as almost all players are from time to time, and that any suggestion that you have deliberately played badly for money is ridiculous?

That may be what you *feel* you want to say. But do you say it? There is a snag – in fact there may be several. You have been playing badly because you have other things on your mind, but if you talk to the media and say that you have other things on your mind, they will inevitably ask you what things. Can you afford to tell them? The things you have had on your mind are that your eleven year-old son has been diagnosed with leukaemia, and that your wife, after years of infidelities, is in the process of leaving you for another man.

If you answer media questions by revealing these facts, the suspicion that you have played badly deliberately may be eased. But it may not be. Might it be thought that, in a state of mind in which you are not quite yourself, you could indeed have accepted bribes? All these possibilities must be sorted out in your mind before you say as much as 'Good morning!' to any reporter.

You must ask yourself what would be the most acceptable course, and rehearse in your mind the possible questions that may well follow from that course. Don't deceive yourself by trying to pretend to yourself that such and such simply can't happen: it probably can, and will. Be thoroughly prepared to answer the questions you wish weren't asked as well as those you want to answer.

These are possible courses:

1 You stay silent and keep your head down, while trying your utmost to improve your performances on the football field.

In this case, reporters and photographers will inevitably pursue you in places where you cannot easily evade them. The reporters will try to get you to comment on the stories that some players have indeed taken bribes.

Course (1) will mean that you will not visit your usual clubs and pubs, will stop your usual early morning jogging exercises, and will enter the gates of your home ground with total silence or a 'no comment' to any media people waiting there.

This will be taxing and tedious, but may be the best course until the names of players who *have* taken bribes emerge, when the heat may well be taken off you. You will have saved yourself having to talk about your son's potentially fatal illness and your coming domestic break-up.

But you will not have endeared yourself to the reporters who have stood around in the rain 'doorstepping' you and having constantly to report failure back to their news desks. They or their news desks may well decide that you have something to hide; that there may well be more bad apples in the barrel to those already revealed – and that you are one of them.

2 You can get your football club to call a press conference or call one yourself, at which you will specifically and in detail answer any questions about the alleged taking of bribes.

This is a high risk move. It may well be that the questions you will be asked will deal purely with the question of bribes and that you may not have to reveal any more personal material. Or you may not be so lucky.

One way or the other, you must beforehand prepare a statement in your head to the effect that you have certainly not been playing at your best lately, but, then, a lot of players go through these troughs and come out the other side. You have never taken any bribe and know of no players who have taken bribes. You are surprised at the stories hinting that you may be involved, but deny categorically that you have been.

To pursue this course successfully, you may have to

reveal all your bank statements to your club officials, so that you can tell the press conference that you have done so. You will say that all your financial affairs are open to inspection by club officials or the police if they want to look – though the police have shown no interest in you so far.

Many of the reporters present will by now have decided that this is a non-story. But almost inevitably there will be one persistent reporter who asks: 'But the standard of your playing has gone down to a greater extent than is usual in players who are just having a bad patch. The other day, you almost shot into your own goal. It was almost as if you were doing it deliberately, or had something else on your mind.'

If you say, 'Yes, I did have other things on my mind,' the reporter will almost certainly follow up with: 'Like what?' Beware, in such circumstances, of the temptation to be facetious. If you say, 'Oh, income tax, my holidays, ingrowing toenails, that sort of thing', you will be asked why you are worried about income tax. You may well have increased the suspicion that the 'sort of thing' that was on your mind when you almost scored an own goal was financial. And if it were, the media people will wonder, wouldn't that be a motive for taking bribes?

Don't be facetious, and certainly don't be facetious off the top of your head. In all encounters with the media it is best to stick as close to the truth as you can.

3   This brings us to another course. You decide to offer a specific explanation of why you were preoccupied when you almost scored that own-goal.

In this case, you must choose one of the real causes – the one you are the least reluctant to reveal – and hope that this will keep the press corps off all other subjects.

You must be quite clear about your personal priorities. You can say that your son has leukaemia, or you can say that your wife is leaving you for another man. Either will do as an explanation for your period of bad playing. Either will create some public sympathy for you, as well as dismissing the suggestion that you may have been playing badly because you were getting backhander payments for it. But revealing both will create a muddle and perhaps promote the suspicion that an honest man would not produce so many excuses.

Assess the pros and cons of each possible announcement.

Will your young son be mortified or gratified to see his name in the newspapers and across the television screens? If he wouldn't mind, then revealing his illness might be the better course. It would not discredit you, nor would it discredit your young son, for such an illness is not discreditable. It would not completely alienate your wife, and it would be at least theoretically possible that before news of your domestic discord leaked out the situation might have mended itself – something that could hardly happen if your wife's personal affairs were revealed by an alienated husband.

But what if the young son *would* mind publicity? Then you might well decide on the other explanation. In this way you would not need to mention him at all but merely to reveal your wife's coming departure for another man. After a married life consisting of her constant infidelities, you might decide that you don't care tuppence for her feelings, whereas you do care about your son's.

Whichever of the two courses you choose, your dealings

with the media should be clear and decisive. The media will demand its bone. Make sure, if you are defending yourself against false accusations or hints, that you throw it a good and conclusive one.

Do not, under almost any circumstances, be so undignified as to drive away in your car shouting to a posse of reporters 'These rumours are ridiculous, and I will consider legal action against anyone repeating them.' The media will react to such an in-flight declaration in two ways. They will say, 'Oh, the rumours are "ridiculous", are they? We shall prove to the contrary!' And the threat of legal action will put them on their mettle. On the whole, people do not threaten legal action if they are innocent (why should they; the truth is surely good enough?). It is easier to think of guilty parties who have threatened to sue the media than it is to think of innocent parties who have actually obtained damages.

As we have seen, the difficulty comes when the truth that would be a convincing defence cannot be revealed without some personal damage. Select the truths you are prepared to discuss with care. Rehearse in your mind the answer to every conceivable question you could be asked, and the answers you would give. The more you rehearse, the more command you will have over your material, and the less you are likely to blurt out more than you need to do.

For example, if as the footballer you, having revealed your son's leukaemia, were then asked by a reporter, 'Is your wife leaving you?' you might get away with an answer like 'When I left home this morning, she was still there having a cup of tea'. This might well produce a general laugh and terminate that line of questioning – while being literally true.

Appear to be especially relaxed when skating near matters you don't want discussed: uneasiness will convey itself to the media as fear will do to a predator. But, equally, if the dreaded question or questions don't come, don't let the relief show in your face and *don't* yourself drift into voluntary comments that concern the dodgy area. (It is amazing how many clever people trip themselves up in this way. It is a form of gambling: how close to the sun can Icarus fly without falling to his death?)

A well-prepared and true answer, based on anticipation of questions you do *not* want asked as well as those you *do* want asked, is at the core of surviving a media interrogation. A good answer in this context is not open-ended: it should appear to end any ambiguity, and it should *not* be added to as an after-thought. (Avoid after-thoughts, because they can be mined territory you have not fully surveyed. Once you have said what you want to say in the way you wanted to say it, shut up, and wait for the next question.)

A popular journalistic technique, especially in one-to-one interviews, is to ask a question, get the answer and then let a long silence develop, so that the person being questioned feels compelled to add to his answer. A long silence can be embarrassing – whose nerve will crack first? Make sure it is not yours. A good journalist cannot afford to be embarrassed, and neither can you.

6 No Script

You are the recently elected spokesman for the residents'
association of a Victorian street which in its heyday was
considered decidedly 'posh'; it still has some architectural
charm, of which long-term residents are proud.

There have lately been suggestions of vandalism, drug-
taking and drug-dealing, burglary and other crimes
committed by newcomers to the street. Some of these
newcomers are Afro-Caribbean, some are Asian, some are
white. Racist grafitti have become common, attacks on
white and ethnic groups not infrequent.

Recently a residents' association was formed. It is not
satisfied with the lighting and policing of the street and
wants better street lamps and a stronger and more visible
police presence in the area. But it is anxious to emphasize
that trouble has arisen in all racial groups, and that its position is not racist. Some members believe that a low public
profile and work behind the scenes is the best answer, but
the majority now feel that a higher public profile is necessary.

A local radio station invites you, as the association's
elected spokesman, to its studio to put your association's

point of view. The subject is highly inflammatory, and the wrong word in the wrong place could have disastrous results. You could be pardoned for scripting your comments and trying to stick to them, and them only, when in the studio.

But don't.

Why not? Because if you do have a script, you will be surprised when you hear a recording of your performance. You will sound indecisive, which is bad. You will sound shifty, which is worse. You will also sound like a hypocrite whose words are not your own, which is worse still.

Having a script in front of you is not a help, it is like trying to ride two horses at once.

Ideally you will try to look the man on the other side of the microphone in the eye, but with a script you will instead find yourself trying to find your place in the script. As an answer to the precise question just asked, a section of your script will almost certainly not be a good fit, so following it will create the impression that you are in some way being evasive and not talking to the point. What are you trying to hide?

Worse still, you may try to scribble an answer to a question before you deliver it, as a sort of mini-script. This will come across to the listener as unaccountable hesitation. Again, what are you trying to hide? If you can't read your own hastily written script and fumble for the right words, things will be worse still. Are you drunk as well, or high on pot yourself? Is the reason that you are so angry about the issue of drug-dealing perhaps because you are a rival drug dealer?

You may seek to blame the interviewer for wrong-footing you in such a case. But the truth will be that it is the very existence of your script which has wrong-footed you. And scripts have another potential disadvantage. Facing a person who is trying to read scripted answers to him may make an interviewer more aggressive. There he is, asking you perfectly reasonable questions, and you are not confident enough of your own case to find original words in which to phrase it!

So what *do* you do, if the subject is touchy? You cannot possibly go in completely unprepared; that would be suicide. You write out notes of key points and how you will explain them, and you memorize them. Once you are confident that you know these points by heart, you put your notes in your pocket and leave them there throughout the interview.

As a compromise, you may produce the notes, possibly with an early off-air apology: 'I'm new to this job, so I've just jotted down one or two points.' But what you *don't* do is anything which suggests that your spiel will be the same whatever questions the interviewer asks. That makes him feel redundant, and he is bound to give you a harder time than he would have done had you appeared to answer his questions spontaneously. (If your positions had been reversed, wouldn't you react the same way?)

The real value of making notes is *not* that you produce and use them during an interview; they may not appear at all. Their value lies in the fact of your having made them. The mental process you have had to go through to do this concentrates your mind wonderfully. With a pen in your hand, you *have* to think clearly and to the point. That is why those who rely on their personability, charm or eccentricity to get through most of life's difficulties are often useless at writing: they have never had to think clearly, and so, when they put pen to paper nothing articulate or convincing happens.

Once you have written out the gist of the main points you want to put across to the media, you can afford to put the notes to one side and rely on the clarity of mind your pen has induced. If you have written down your points slowly and carefully, you will easily know which point to produce in answer to which question.

This is the best way to produce a sense of spontaneity while being absolutely sure of what you want to say. If that comforting thought still leaves you lacking in confidence, then by all means condense your key points to the minimum of words, list them on a single sheet of paper and have that list in front of you on the studio table as you speak. But listen carefully to the interviewer's questions, and only glance at the notes if you *have* to – because, say, nervousness has made you temporarily forget the answer to a particular point.

In some sorts of interview – where no studio table is present – you would not be able to produce even a list of points, let alone a script. Trapped in the street with a microphone under your nose, for instance, you would not want to fiddle in your pockets for bits of paper. It would look tacky and shifty.

It is true that some solicitors representing clients involved in newsworthy court cases have got into the habit of reading out statements from the court precincts. This practice may be pardoned if it is on behalf of someone else – a solicitor may well create sympathy by reading out: 'My client has great sympathy with the widow of the man he knocked over and, though he still denies any wrong-doing and will appeal, he has offered to pay the medical expenses of the child whose leg was broken.' But imagine the defendant himself appearing outside the court and reading out the same statement in the first person. The reaction of the public might well be: 'So I suppose you think everything's all right now?'

The existence of a script, or something that suggests the existence of a script, is more likely to trip you up than assist you when confronting the media in any shape or form. Mastery of the subject, so that all its elements are familiar to you and ready in your mind, is a far better survival kit.

7 Don't Run

If a mouse kept perfectly still, it just might be safe from a cat. In fact it runs away, with the cat in hot (and probably successful) pursuit. There is a lesson here for people who are sought out by the media: it is vital not to give the *appearance* of running away or trying to hide. To the cat or the media, running will signal that pursuit – possibly a humiliating pursuit – is not only justified but actively called for.

Watch defendants covering their faces with their hands or a newspaper as they go into the court. They may simply feel overwhelmed by the number of media people on the pavement outside the court; they may feel persecuted and, out of spite, try to ruin the media cameramen's work; they may be covering their faces for all sorts of reasons that appear to them to be absolutely sensible. But what *impression* does their action convey? That of furtiveness, evasiveness, *guilt*.

Watch an inexperienced politician going into some important meeting in London, Brussels or Washington. He shields the side of his face with his hand as he runs the gauntlet of media cameras and media notebooks. He may have cut himself while shaving and be trying to hide the ugly scab; he may want no footage or column inches about himself to be used until after the meeting, when he hopes he will have something positive to say that will cast him in a good light; he may have all sorts of motives for shielding his face. But the impression left on the public is one of furtiveness or secrecy – the very things a politician should not suggest by his personal manner.

It may be politic for all sorts of people – presidents, prime ministers, captains of industry or of labour, spokesmen for controversial bodies, or ordinary members of the public – to avoid the media at certain times. But, if it is to be effective at all, that avoidance should be absolute: in other words, the person should make sure, as far as they are able, that they go nowhere near any media representatives. If this is impossible, because paths they must take in the course of daily life and work can be monitored by the media, then they should not appear evasive but give the impression of taking the media candidly, head-on.

The politician should smile nicely or adopt an expression of extreme gravitas, according to the mood of the moment. He should say to the waiting reporters and cameramen: 'Sorry, I can't say anything at this stage; you will understand that a lot depends on today's meeting. But afterwards I will be pleased to talk to you.' He should then turn and walk towards his meeting, appearing not to hear shouted questions.

By this course of action, he will have made several things clear. First, he has a rational reason for not, at that time, talking at length to the media people who are besieging him. Second, by making that brief comment he has registered the fact, or at least the impression, that he has no hostility to the media as such. Third, he has made a concrete promise to talk more fully later – a tactic that should keep any potential rebels within the media corps quiet.

At no stage has he – or should he have – suggested that he was fleeing from cameras or notebooks. On the contrary he actively took them into consideration rather than avoided them, explaining reasonably why he couldn't say anything at that particular time. Nothing in his manner or behaviour suggested fear or flight.

When he leaves the critical meeting, which may not have been as satisfactory as he had hoped, he has a further choice to make. One option is to leave by the back door and avoid as many journalists as possible. This will be noted and commented on vigorously by the media, who will feel cheated (though the public might conceivably sympathize with him rather than his pursuers), and he will have lost a chance to explain to the public in his own terms what has happened.

It will almost certainly be far better if he decides to leave as publicly as he arrived, to explain succinctly how and why the meeting was not as satisfactory as he had hoped, and then to exit with the explanation that saying more at this stage might complicate things further and lessen chances of agreement.

The behaviour of the fictional politician has lessons for all sorts of people who may be intimidated by the thought of showing their faces to the media. It is better to fight than to fear, better to have a brief statement ready in your head than to weave and dodge publicly in the hope of having to say nothing.

In some circumstances the more boring that statement is,

the better – it may then never be used in any news coverage. This in effect preserves the anonymity you seek, but which you would *not* gain by fleeing like a mouse from a cat, or doing something that could appear to be running away.

But non-flight does require a degree of nerve that some people may find difficult to summon up. In nine cases out of ten, especially in less dramatic situations which are more typical of relations with the media, it helps to bear well in mind that you know far more about the subject at issue than your questioner does (else why would he be asking you questions?), and that his difficult question may not be a trap for you as much as a genuine request for enlightenment.

In such circumstances you may still treat his question with caution, even extreme caution. But you will not be disturbed by the paranoid thought that someone is 'out to get you'. You will say to yourself, 'Is there any real reason why I can't answer his question?' If the answer to this is an unencouraging, 'Yes!', you can go on to ask yourself, 'Can I briefly and in general terms explain *why* at this stage I can't answer the question?' If the answer to this is again 'Yes,' the rest depends on the speed at which you can think on your feet (assuming you didn't anticipate the encounter and rehearse your answers to all approaches, as you should have done). Deliver your brief explanation for your silence, smile and firmly walk on or, in a static situation like a press conference or a one-to-one interview, politely seek a change of subject.

Provided you give the impression in such circumstances of *trying* to be helpful, you will tend to keep the media and the public 'on side' as far as you personally are concerned.

Any irritated blows will tend to fall on other people, which (if you can comfortably take such a *realpolitik* point of view) may be bad for them but will be good for you.

The concept of *realpolitik* may suggest another practice which can sometimes be regarded as an alternative to fleeing media 'intrusion'. If the media is hot on your heels for a story of your alleged misdoings, tipping them off about an even better story concerning another person is a tactic that has been tried. This, to put it bluntly and simply, is immoral. That may or may not disturb you, but you will certainly be disturbed by the thought that it may not work.

The section of the media which is after you may well thank you kindly for your news tip about the other person and then go on pursuing you nonetheless. What will you be able to do then? Go public about the betrayal? Hardly! And even if that section of the media keeps faith with you, you may still be exposed by other sections of the media. And, if the person you sneaked on has any inkling that you were behind it, you will have gained an enemy who may be patiently determined to do you an injury however long it takes.

Honesty can be the best policy. In fact, be as honest as you can, and always *behave* as if you are honest – which usually precludes all thoughts of running away or appearing to run away.

8   Be Prepared

Unexpectedly being asked for a comment by the media when you knew its representatives were in the vicinity but thought that you personally were not 'in the line of fire' can be an uncomfortable experience. The remedy is to anticipate events and have your response ready whenever you attend an event where the media may be present, whether or not you expect to be called upon to make a comment.

This will be easier in some circumstances than in others.

Let us suppose, for example, that you are a guest at the memorial service – or 'ceremony of thanksgiving' as they are sometimes called in a secular age – for a person well-known nationally or locally. You have not been to such a service before and don't know the form. You will find that after the service members of the congregation/audience tend to stand around outside the venue chatting to one another, and perhaps talking to any reporters covering the story who may approach them. You are one of the lesser-known people there and don't expect to be approached (many reporters present may not know who you are), but the reporter of a quality daily newspaper approaches you and asks for your view of the deceased. He is obviously trying to build up a feature on the event rather than merely reporting what was said and what happened in the church or other venue.

In the space of a microsecond, you have to make up your mind what your priorities are. Do you want to be invisible, or do you want to be quoted? Your respect for the deceased may be such that you feel you simply must utter some words of praise. In that case you know your motive, you know that it is not self-interest, and you know that any trouble is something that you will simply take in your stride. But if you have no such powerful sentiment, the criterion should be: what course would best serve your interests?

If the deceased was an eminent musician, and you are a humble if promising music teacher, it might well serve your interests to be quoted in a report of his memorial service. It might just possibly help you to become a rather less humble music teacher, if devotees of the deceased consider your remarks worthy and well chosen.

If you are comparatively low in the professional hierarchy but anxious to be quoted, you should certainly take care to make your brief remark or remarks interesting and unconventional – the sort of thing that the journalist may prefer to a blander comment from someone better known. You may utter only one or two sentences, but those should be arresting in their sentiments and their wording. Find an original word, one that no one else is likely to use, and you may find your brief comments quoted while those of better-known people are not.

On the other hand, producing such a well rehearsed throw-away line may not produce a profitable outcome.

There may be those in the music field who will say to themselves 'I am far better qualified to give an opinion than him!' Others may say 'He is getting above himself!', or 'That wasn't the essence of the man we have just paid tribute to. He is talking rot!' There may even be those above you in your own hierarchy who believe that no such lowly practitioner should be allowed to open his mouth.

If you decide that (a) your respect for the deceased is such that you must record it by attending his memorial service, but (b) it would be unwise of you to open your mouth in any way whatever, what do you do?

You identify the reporters covering the event and make sure it is never easy to approach you, or – to put it another way – that it is always easier to approach someone else. This means you keep physically as far away from the journalists as you can. Alternatively, if this is difficult to do because they are all over the place, you always keep close to different celebrities who are far more worth talking to than you are. (If you are a junior politician, you are fairly safe if you keep ten feet away from the Prime Minister, Chancellor of the Exchequer or Foreign Secretary. Everyone will be after them and will hardly notice your presence, let alone try to talk to you). In this way celebrity hunting, which has become an increasingly desperate activity in media circles, can sometimes work to your advantage if you don't want to be quoted or would ideally prefer to be totally invisible.

But supposing there are no big celebrities present to draw off attention, and the media is reduced to interviewing the second or third division teams – which includes you? It is possible to elude a pursuing journalist in such circumstances, by simply and literally being faster on your feet than he is, while making sure that your movements appear to be accidental. This is a rather undignified process, though, more suited to the gyrations of the ballroom than a memorial service or similar event. And if you are not a good enough actor, and your evasion becomes suspected, it may make the journalist wonder why you are avoiding him (is some dark secret about you about to emerge?). You will then be pin-pointed with more fervour.

Appearing to run away is therefore rarely if ever a wise tactic. It is probably better to do what you should do in all cases: have ready a well-rehearsed comment that you can produce as if it is spontaneous. However, in this particular case – when you don't want to irritate colleagues by having your name and views prominently in print – you say something like, 'He was very nice' several times in a boring uninflected voice and pass on. The journalist will have no difficulty crossing this banality out of his notebook. If you don't want to be quoted but have no public-interest reason you can advance for not being quoted, it often pays to be as boring as possible. Say little, and that halting and banal. Or say a lot, in a dreary voice and none of it vivid or interesting, until the journalist's eyes glaze over and he moves on to someone else. In either case, he almost certainly will not want to quote such a bore.

Do not go into *any* situation in which the media will or may be present without rehearsing either what you will say if asked or how you will evade any journalistic interest. It should not take you too long to string two sentences together and polish them, and then, as a reserve, string another two together and polish them as well. If you want a journalist to keep clear of you whenever he sees you, do the same thing with even more sentences, each more

tedious than the last. This is a high-risk move – the journalist may just possibly like the trite and banal – but it has
been tried by people with strong nerves.

9   One or Several?

You have something you wish to convey to the media. Do you call a press conference and invite all the sections of the media that could possibly be interested? Or do you ring selected individual journalists and offer them interviews on a one-to-one basis?

It depends on the nature of the material and the nature of your relationship with those journalists you would seek to interest. If the material is specialized, you may wish to discuss it quietly and in detail. If, as is likely, you know the specialist journalists who cover that area, there is a strong case for focusing on them individually. Also, if only two or three journalists could possibly be interested, it would pay you to telephone each of them and arrange appointments at different times. But not only should the times be different, they should be generously spaced out, so that if you over-run your time with journalist A, he does not on his way out meet journalist B coming in. (In such circumstances journalist B is likely to feel that he is an afterthought, especially if he happens to dislike or is jealous of journalist A.)

You should do everything in your power to foster the impression that you are treating everyone equally, even if you are not. In particular, even if you attach more importance to a minute on television than to a column in a newspaper, you should take care not to allow this to show in your dealings with newspaper people, who will be sensitive about the relative power of television and print. It will almost certainly be easier to negotiate this potentially fraught situation if you see journalists individually than if you call a press conference.

The danger of calling a press conference, especially to deal with a controversial subject, is that it could be transformed, in effect, into a television studio, with the newspaper and magazine journalists acting as unpaid film extras – a role they may not like. If you can deal with television and the press quite separately, so much the better.

From your point of view as distinct from that of the journalists', the main advantage of a press conference is that, if the subject is a broad one of interest to a lot of journalists, it saves time. You will not be asked precisely the same question two, three or even twenty times. Neither will you unintentionally give a better answer to journalist A than to rival journalist B. If they are paying attention, both A and B will hear the same answer (and, if they are not, they will have only themselves to blame).

Strangely, a sensitive subject on which you wish to say as little as possible is often more easily dealt with at a press conference than by contact with individual journalists on a one-to-one basis. When facing an individual journalist in a one-to-one encounter, you will have nowhere to hide if his questions become too pressing, but by manipulating a press conference it is often possible to escape, or at least blunt, difficult questions.

One way of doing this is to give the briefest possible answer to an awkward question and then suddenly notice another journalist 'who has had his hand up for some time' and ask him for his question (there will almost certainly be no lack of journalists who want to ask questions). In this way you make evasion look and sound like an attempt to be even-handed with all the journalists present.

Simply not noticing a journalist who you know is about to ask an awkward question is a useful technique, but it can backfire: you can't fail to notice any journalist for ever, and by the time you have to notice him he will probably be feeling even more belligerent than he did when he first put up his hand. Moreover, not taking notice of a potential questioner works only so long as the journalist concerned observes the etiquette of waiting to be called. But, if he has a powerful voice and is determined to use it, he can merely project his question *without* first being called – a practice most journalists have resorted to at some time.

All the same, a difficult customer at a press conference is up against limitations he would not suffer if you faced him one-to-one. Lengthy questioning can be dodged on the grounds that it is self-centred and unfair to the other journalists present.

Should you stay behind after a press conference to chat to any individual journalist who approaches you? This is often done, but, if the subject is sensitive, it may vitiate the benefits of a press conference from your point of view. There is something to be said in such circumstances for leaving the platform and disappearing with all the other speakers.

The advantage of staying is that you can round off or confirm complex points to any interested journalist. For example, individual journalists from regional newspapers and radio stations may hope to develop local angles on the subject you have been talking about, and if you stay they may be able to do this without standing on their colleagues' toes or yours.

The disadvantage is that journalists may tend not to ask important and news-worthy questions at the press conference itself (where, of course, they and the answers can be heard by rivals) but in the ensuing free-for-all. The result can be that one journalist gets a better story than the rest, and the rest will be resentful and may blame you. In future their attitude may be, 'Why bother to attend your press conferences, when in fact you give better stories out in private briefings?'

If, after a press conference, you think that individual journalist A has gained a better story than anyone else through chatting to you, you are free to telephone his peers journalists B and C and tip them off on the point, pleading that you had simply overlooked it at the formal press conference. This will endear you to them, but not to journalist A if he finds out about it – which, journalists being great gossips, he probably will. He is likely to take the view that you have spoiled a scoop which he obtained through his own initiative.

On the whole, and with all its risks, contact with individual journalists on a one-to-one basis is likely to be the most effective way of putting a story across. Especially with television cameras present, press conferences have tended to mutate into something like formal state occasions at which august personages have the chance to sound off and look good, rather than be a source of real stories. Increasingly, therefore, journalists tend to use them as the springboard for their own later one-to-one questioning. From your point of view, this removes one of the advantages of holding the press conference in the first place.

There is a further possibility of difficulty if you operate on a regional or local basis rather than a national one. Let us suppose you have to organize a press conference for a public body which wants to make (for it) an important announcement: you approach all the newspapers, television and radio stations in the area separately, hoping to get as big a turn-out of journalists as possible. But you may not have allowed for the fact that more and more newspapers are owned by one group and, accountant-led, economize by sending only one journalist to press conferences. Instead of facing half a dozen or more journalists, you and your speakers may be in danger of ignominiously being faced with only one or two. Meanwhile, your organization may have decided to field the strongest team it can, including the president, the chairman, their wives, and half a dozen officials. You could end up with far more people on the platform than journalists in the body of the hall. Everyone is likely to find this faintly embarrassing, or at least curious, and if you have been responsible for the arrangements, the odium will fall on you.

At local or regional level, where everyone tends to know everyone else, interviews with individual journalists are likely to offer the best results and the fewest possible embarrassments. Many organizations in the private and public sectors no longer think about calling a press conference unless they are sure that what they want to talk about has the makings of a very big story.

Two advantages of the press conference which remain are the saving of time and the status of the press conference as an insurance policy: unless you forget to invite someone, you can always plead with any malcontent who didn't attend and failed to get a story that you called a press conference and that everyone had their chance to get any story going.

Even when a press conference is held, more and more adroit communications practitioners are calling it something else. The term 'conference' implies that it is a talking shop at which every self-respecting person connected with the subject must be present to (a) meet the journalists personally, and (b) to sustain his reputation inside and outside the organization by talking as much as possible, even when journalists start to fidget.

Often press conferences have been renamed press briefings, with mutual benefits. Fewer members of your organization may insist on attending, which will make for brevity and clarity. And journalists who might have been tempted to give a conference (talking shop) a miss will more readily turn up at something called a briefing, a term which suggests a crisp and succinct handing over of hard facts, rather than a festival of oratory.

In summary, consider calling a press conference or group briefing if:

1. You have something to announce that is really big in journalists' terms as well as your own.
2. So many journalists are likely to be interested in the subject that giving them individual briefings would be prohibitive in terms of time.
3. If there is an emergency in which you regard it as essential to keep control of the emergence of information. (But even in this case you may wish to call the proceedings a briefing rather than a press conference.)

Consider individual briefings if:

1. Only a few specialist journalists are likely to be interested.
2. If, for your own reasons, you want to channel the information through specific parts of the media rather than others.
3. If you want to explain complex matters in detail without putting yourself and experts under too much public pressure.
4. If you think questioning on the information you wish to impart might lead to a public press conference getting out of hand and becoming an embarrassing shambles.

10   Play the Fairness Card

'It simply isn't fair!' All children and many adults expect life to be fair, or at least profoundly hope it will be, for fairness has a high-ranking place in the human mind. In postcolonial times English cricket may not still be the international emblem of all fair dealing, but the concept of fairness is certainly still at the forefront of British and other national consciousnesses.

One of the most potent ways to defend a disputed, contentious and hard policy or course of action is therefore not to attempt to deny its painfulness but to claim that it is fair. If this card can be played, almost any measure has a sporting chance. Could a spokesman justify a policy giving everyone spectacles with one opaque lens on the grounds that it was fair to those who had lost an eye? Perhaps not. But a cynic might claim that no other grounds for introducing such a policy would have a *better* chance of success.

Under the umbrella of 'fairness', high-rise council housing has been introduced to high-priced residential areas, punitive parking rates have been arrived at, and the quality of public services allowed to deteriorate on the grounds that 'in fairness' the money is needed elsewhere.

After the privatisation of water suppliers in Britain, the commercial companies who took over controversially set out to introduce the metering of water, which would lead to many consumers having to pay more. What could be the motive for such a move?

Opponents would (and did) say immediately that it was naked greed on the part of the new companies. Nobody could deny the simple fact that the object of any business (except those registered as non-profit-making) is to maximize profits – and, in an era when the whole concept of service has become blurred, it would also be hard to deny the notion that profits should be based simply on providing a service has become equally blurred.

The new water undertakings set themselves up as targets by the methods they used to get meters in place. In some areas they wrote to householders saying that henceforth no householder could use a garden hose or sprinkler unless his home was fitted with a water meter, which would be fitted free; and if a house was sold without a meter, the new owner would not be accepted as a customer unless he had one fitted. Water meters would at the present time be fitted free, though it was possible that charges would be imposed later.

Some consumers thought this approach amounted to blatant arm-twisting, since it meant that, unless you had a water meter fitted, you couldn't water your garden or clean your car efficiently, and you couldn't sell your house so easily because the buyer would know he would have to have a meter installed, possibly at substantial cost.

How could such an approach be defended? How could metering as a whole be defended? In the main, water company spokesmen ignored all criticism which they would have found difficult to answer and played the fairness card. The argument went something like this. Yes, in all such changes, some won and some lost. A lot of people who used a lot of water would pay more if they were metered, but a lot of people with low water consumption – including old people living alone – would pay considerably less. Wasn't that fair? Wasn't it fair that people who used less water should pay less, and not in effect subsidize fellow consumers who used more, which is what they were doing under the water-rate system?

Seen in that light, the argument for metering was considerably strengthened and the 'strong-arm' methods used to foist the meters on the public were more easily seen as justifiable.

However unattractive the measure you are trying to introduce, the step you are trying to take, or the case you have to defend, try to find some element of fairness in it. And concentrate on playing that fairness card for all you are worth, sidelining some of the other less attractive points as much as possible. This is an effective way of glossing a difficult case (though not the only one).

The central point to bear in mind is this. It is usually a mistake to try to ignore or brush aside the difficult points of your case. The technique is to acknowledge them as 'problems', rather than unqualified disasters. You need to regard them as something like uncomfortable spikes sticking out of your case and to centre your defence on smoothing down these spikes as much as possible, and not to insult the intelligence of the public by trying to behave as if they were not there.

You should not expect this to be easy, especially if the issue is an emotive one, and the difficulty is as great for the secretary of a bee-keeping club defending a traditional inner-city site for a bee colony as it is for a government minister defending proposed legislation. Nonetheless, for every difficulty, try to find a balancing virtue to help wear away those difficult spikes.

The technique may come more easily to seasoned politicians dealing with big public issues than to inexperienced secretaries of inner-city bee-keeping societies, but even the inexperienced spokesmen at local level can certainly learn a lot from the experienced politician about how to minimize what cannot be denied, and how to smooth out the threatening spikes in any proposal or argument. An appeal to fairness can certainly be one of the most formidable instruments of that process.

11 No 'Perspective'

Imagine yourself in the following situation. British Railways has been broken up, different private operators are running trains in different parts of the country for commercial profit, and the directors of some of them are paying themselves increased salaries while profits flag and the service deteriorates. Then a report by an independent body appears. It castigates the quality of service and suggests that, if it does not improve radically and soon, franchises should be taken away from companies doing especially badly and handed to other operators.

The situation becomes an inflamed public issue. A BBC or commercial radio station decides to do a programme on the situation. Its reporters travel on services run by heavily criticized companies, putting together horror stories from fellow travellers who talk about long delays, sudden withdrawal of trains, breakdowns, signal failures and other irritants. Their stories, often delivered with considerable heat and even rudeness, are used at the start of the programme, and then the presenter of the programme begins to question spokesmen of the criticized companies. One of those is you.

What do you do? Fall on your sword? That would be a

once-only solution. Even so, it might be better than some of the responses that company spokesmen could adopt.

What you do *not* do in such circumstances is to criticize the BBC or the commercial station for broadcasting an 'alarmist' or 'sensationalized' programme. If you do, five hundred or more people will immediately ring your train operating company to say that it is ignorant of what is really going on as well as incompetent; that its three-piece-suited chairman (if he can tear himself away from the contemplation of his share options) should try actually travelling on his ghastly trains – then he would see that conditions are actually twice or three times as bad as the programme suggested.

Never criticize the media for doing its job, even if you genuinely believe that the results of its doing so are unfair in a particular case. That will only add a further crime to your bulging dossier: trying to bully and curtail free speech.

Beware of the term 'alarmist'. It will immediately introduce the concept of 'alarm' (which may not so far have been mentioned) and suggest to the listener that there certainly *are* grounds for alarm if you are so eager to deny the criticism. What would *your* reaction be, if you were having a pleasant dinner in a restaurant and the chef suddenly ran in and shouted, 'The food is not poisoned!'? You would not be reassured; on the contrary, you would very probably assume there was a distinct possibility that the food *had* been poisoned.

Avoid using dramatic or melodramatic terms with a pejorative meaning, even in attempted refutation. The media will be delighted if you use such phrases, because dramatic words and phrases grab the ears of listeners and sell newspapers. They are a fox that the media – quite legitimately from its point of view – will infallibly chase.

Similarly, it may be wise to avoid using even dramatic terms that carry a favourable meaning. This may seem surprising, but yesterday's florid self-praise may be tomorrow's stick to beat you with. Suppose, for example, that the rail company spokesman had answered the criticisms by saying 'We are rapidly improving our service and are heading for a new dawn'.

The phrase 'new dawn' might seem appropriate, because it can be picked up and used in a headline or sound bite. Perhaps it will be; perhaps also, with the passage of time an improvement in services will justify its use. Remember that the media sometimes follows up stories (not often enough but sometimes), and in a case with a high public profile such as this it is very likely that, say, a year after the 'new dawn' was promised, they will do another test of services. If they find the services have *not* improved, they will use the 'new dawn' phrase to describe the rail company concerned – just as Neville Chamberlain, who promised 'peace in our time' when he returned from Munich in 1938, was derided when war broke out in 1939.

What you also do *not* do in the situation we are discussing is to dispute the criticisms of the travellers interviewed for the critical programme. They are already irritated by your company's shortcomings, and the last thing they need to be told is that they are lying, imagining things or exaggerating. If you, as a company spokesman, do dispute their evidence (unless, of course, you have absolutely watertight reasons for doing so), this will almost certainly provoke other witnesses to come forward with even more damning evidence, and the situation from your point of view will be worse rather than better.

The best you can do will probably be to put the conditions in perspective *without* ever using that phrase. Why not use it? Because its use will be highly irritating to sufferers. If people arrived late at work three times in one week because their 'regular' train has been delayed or cancelled, it will be absolutely maddening to hear some plummy-voiced public relations man (that is how irritated sufferers will almost inevitably see or hear you) ask them to 'put this into perspective – 51 per cent of our trains do run on time'.

The public, realistically or not, wants perfection: 100 per cent of trains running on time. It will certainly not be won over by the fact that 51 per cent of them do so – especially not those who happen to have been travelling on the other 49 per cent. It is no good trying to talk away inadequacies by use of the phrase 'putting the facts into perspective' – the very sound of the word 'perspective' is enough to inflame any sufferer.

What you should do is indeed to put the facts into perspective – but *without* ever using that alarming and irritating phrase. Faced with the dossier of complaints from the public, you should immediately say that you sympathize and are doing everything possible to remedy the situation. Then you explain that the railway service was in a very run-down state before being taken over by private companies, and that all private companies are having difficulties making good years of neglect. You go on to point out that the improvement programmes of all private companies were always understood to be on a three- or four-year basis, and that there are several years yet to go. Some complainants may dismiss this as 'jam tomorrow', but the more reasonable of them are likely to accept the point and not judge the companies finally until the full improvement term is up.

At this point the spokesman is almost inevitably going to be reminded by the interviewer that the government has power to remove franchises from companies that do not perform well, and asked: 'Wouldn't it put some gunpowder under all the companies if one or two of them had their franchises taken away from them?' ('Too right!' will be the instinctive reaction of many listeners, who will think the point self-evident.)

How is any spokesman to react to this question without irritating the public further? He should *not* dispute the suggestion head on and say, 'No, that would be going altogether too far.' ('Too far?', one can hear listeners echoing sarcastically. 'Too far! What mealy-mouthed rubbish! It doesn't go far enough! Take the franchises away from the lot!') What he can more safely say is: 'I think most reasonable travellers would accept that talk about putting gunpowder under people is not helpful. What the situation requires is a determined attempt by companies like ours to pursue our improvement plans with vigour over a period of three or four years, and that is what we are doing.' Then the spokesman could legitimately list the improvements made so far and the improvements that will be made in the next year, quoting specifics. (This would be done, as it were, under the umbrella of disputing dramatic language.)

In that context most reasonable members of the public might regard the argument as acceptable – whereas, if the spokesman had begun his response by listing all the marvellous things his company was doing, the immediate memory of the complaints themselves would quite likely have led to their being brushed aside.

Seek perspective, but without saying that is what you are doing. And even then do not be in too much of a hurry to do it, or you may be regarded as merely glib.

12 Seek General-interest Points

If you want to get an idea, a product or a policy across effectively, try to see and project it in the broadest possible terms, not just your own. Ideally your subject would be presented so that it seemed to touch the lives of everybody. This will not in practice be possible, but it should certainly seem to be as unlike a self-serving scam as possible.

People who have developed something to sell – be it a policy or a product – tend to be a little fanatical; they tend to live, eat and breathe their own subject. This may be fine from the point of view of developing a product or policy, but it can be lethal from the point of view of putting it across to journalists and, through them, the public.

Such zealots are rather like those computer instructors so in love with the technology of the equipment they are discussing that they explain to new students the thousand and one things the equipment *can* do without ever asking themselves what the students actually *want* to do – and what they therefore need to know.

Like those students, you may not need to know the chemical composition of a new patent medicine: you need to know if it will cure your backache. (After all, thousands of people suffer from backache, but only a few are interested in, or qualified to judge, chemical constituents). Therefore, any press releases, briefings and press conferences for the mythical new patent medicine (unless for the specialist media, who in practice may have broken the story first) should concentrate on the potential benefits for sufferers, rather than the no doubt fascinating and worthy story of how the product came to be invented and what its chemical composition is.

How quickly does the new medicine work? Can it be used as a preventative as well as a cure? Does it have any side-effects? Does it work for everybody or nearly everybody? In such a case the presentation should be aimed at the widest possible audience and its benevolent aspects should be emphasized.

One of the few exceptions would be if the story of the development of the product was itself of human interest. If its originator had a bad back, failed to find any cure until an accidental sting from a rare insect mysteriously cured it, and then diligently began analysing the chemical composition of the insect's sting, then that might well find its way into tabloid newspapers as well as specialist magazines. You would be well advised to bring such a story out and feed it to the largest possible sectors of the media.

Such cases are comparatively rare. The public (except perhaps the stock market and the media which cater expressly for it) does not want to know how much money *you* are going to make out of the new idea. It wants to know how that idea will affect *them*, how much richer it will make *their* lives.

Any idea, political, medical, social or merely cosmetic,

should be broadened out as much as possible and its public benevolence emphasized. However, the media has become so good at asking 'What's in it for YOU?' that it has become a cliché, and it is widely assumed that no one does anything except for their own advantage. This has made it more difficult to convince anyone in the media that you are doing something for someone else, which may include the general public.

If you represent a firm of wheel clampers that has just invented a new sort of wheel clamp which can be put in place in half the time, you will have a job convincing anybody that anyone is going to benefit from it except you and your company.

Of course, halving the time needed to attach a wheel clamp will enable your wardens to clamp twice as many vehicles in the same time, thus producing more revenue, and this will endear your firm to local authorities anxious to maximize their revenues from car clamping. That side of the argument cannot be simply wished away, and as the spokesman of such a company, or as the inventor attending the launch press conference, you may as well not attempt to deny it; that would be futile.

What you must do to redress the balance is to marshal facts and arguments to bring out the public benefits that the device will have. For instance, you could argue that if it takes less time to clamp a wheel, the firm's charges to public authorities could be pegged if not reduced. It could also be maintained that taking the least possible time to clamp a wheel would mean less chance of an irate illicit parker arriving during the process and starting a violent argument that might in some cases lead to personal violence. It would also be possible to point out that, if it takes less time to clamp a wheel, it also takes less time to de-clamp it.

Critics of the proposal might well feel that these arguments were insubstantial. If you feel inclined to agree with them (as in this mythical case you probably would), your best course will almost certainly be to make no announcement of any kind, but to have your best possible justification ready in case you are approached. This needs to be substantial enough to at least fudge the accusation that your company is merely out to maximize its profits rather than to serve the public.

Let your arguments be as unegotistical and as little self-serving as possible. Even Mother Teresa did not escape criticism during and after her lifetime. Nonetheless, she received less than estate agents, stockbrokers, politicians or journalists. Why? Because she was perceived as serving the needs of others rather than her own. That perception can be valuable even to the less saintly.

13   Who Speaks?

Sometimes the success of an encounter with the media does not rest entirely on what is said, but on *who* says it. Whether you are a politician advocating a difficult policy, the chairman of a public company defending your faltering balance sheet or a single mother resisting eviction from a council flat, you should think very carefully about whether you should face the media yourself, or whether someone else could do it better for you.

It may not in practice be possible to play things the way you would ideally like them to be played, but you should certainly form a view of what the ideal way is, and then try to see if that can be implemented to some degree, even if not totally.

Remember that the higher in the hierarchy the speaker is, the greater may be the suggestion that matters of great moment – perhaps a series of disasters that must be explained away at highest level – are at hand. During the Kosovo conflict, the 19 NATO countries who were acting against Serbia had various divisions of opinion. For instance, Britain was obviously more in favour of a ground invasion than many other members, including America – and during this time the number of publicized meetings between the British Prime Minister and the American President was wisely kept to a minimum. Broadly, they shared a platform only at times when the answers to the questions they were likely to be asked were ones they were agreed upon.

At other times, they left speaking to the media to their respective heads of foreign affairs or to other spokesmen. It was these subordinates, rather than the number one men, who had a three-way conversation with a BBC radio interviewer at the height of the ground troops dispute. If the number one men had been fielded in such a situation, this would have carried the suggestion that disagreements were so serious that they could only be dealt with at top level. Their very presence might have subliminally said: 'The situation is not only serious but desperate.'

The same principle applies right down the political, social and commercial scale – but with the proviso that, if there is a point at issue that visibly only the number one man can deal with, then he may be thought guilty of personal evasion if he does not face the media personally.

A public company defending its balance sheet might get away with fielding the Finance Director. If it did that, rather than putting forward the Chairman or Chief Executive, it might succeed in subliminally suggesting to the public that the bad financial results were somehow a matter of book-keeping rather than essential market weakness.

But putting forward the Corporate Affairs Director – a title which usually means PR person with a seat on the board – might be more controversial. Such people can no doubt be valuable executives at an internal advisory level, but their appearance as public spokesmen can give the impression that the monkey is performing because the organ grinder is dodging a virtually certain hostile public reaction. Some adroit corporate affairs directors or their equivalents would urge their chairmen or chief executives in nine cases out of ten to do difficult interviews personally, after being carefully briefed about the sort of questions likely to be asked and the sort of answers most likely to satisfy questioners.

The case of a fictional single mother resisting eviction from a council flat might not be as different as might be supposed. Wouldn't, say, a solicitor put over her case better than she could? It could be argued that she would be likely to come off worst in any exchange with the media, and that therefore someone else should speak for her.

But this pessimistic crystal ball often lies. Sometimes human simplicity, or the appearance of simplicity, can win the public over more effectively than patent sophistry. Certainly, if legal assistance were available, she might be able to speak through a solicitor when dealing with the print and electronic media. But, if she did, some readers or listeners might wonder what she had to hide.

For the parties to a crisis, controversy or dispute, large or small, the case in favour of facing the media themselves, rather than sheltering behind professional spokesmen, is simple. It is the same as the argument for urging a defendant in a court case *not* to throw a blanket over his head: such a quest for invisibility can immediately suggest guilt, even if the person concerned is innocent.

In the case of the single mother facing eviction, she would almost certainly be wiser to face the media herself, rather than to let anyone else speak for her. She should certainly not let her unemployed and shaven-headed boyfriend and cohabitee, who may be part of the reason for the council's attitude, speak for her.

In general, information is most convincing when it comes from the horse's mouth. It is certainly best not to hand over to someone else merely because you are inexpert at handling the media; if you do, you will never become expert. It is better to learn how to deal with the media by trial and error, practising, if you can contrive it, when the stakes are low rather than high.

The main exception to this, at the corporate level, is when the presence of the top man might suggest that matters are even more serious than they are. Otherwise, the more the public can feel it is in touch with the actual parties to a dispute, or those who are actually responsible for decisions, rather than their spokesmen, the better.

14 Staying Silent

There are a relatively small number of occasions when it is best to maintain silence in the face of the media, but they do exist.

Imagine that a number of people have been affected by a poisoning outbreak in a seaside resort, and that there have also been stories in that vicinity of refuse and sewage floating in the sea. You are the press officer to the local council (or the chairman of its public health or other relevant committee, the leader of the council, the spokesman for the Environment Agency – or, indeed, anyone who could be held to be responsible for the outbreak or in some way connected with its cause).

Obviously, in such a situation it will be vital to let the public have all the *facts* that have been established about the outbreak as soon as possible. Otherwise, rumour will undoubtedly take over, probably multiplying the actual number of cases of poisoning. The facts will be best released through the 'official channels' rather than as quotes from the mouth of a particular individual. Such an individual could become the focus of media hostility.

But it is inevitable that, in such a case, the media's interest will not stop at the accepted facts, especially when the number of poisoning cases is increasing day by day. *How* were the people poisoned? Eventually the medical experts who have treated victims of the outbreak arrive at the conclusion that they were all suffering from *E.coli* infection. Obviously this *fact* will be released to the media as soon as possible, again as from a corporate source rather than from any individual.

But then the media will want to know how the victims came to be infected with *E.coli*. Isn't it true that untreated sewage and other refuse have been seen on beaches at the resort? Are bathers on these beaches at risk? And isn't it a fact that beefburgers sold by seaside stalls could also be a possible cause of the outbreak?

Here we have all the makings of a story which could be highly damaging to the seaside resort and its commerce, especially when one of the *E.coli* sufferers dies. By questioning the victims and by medical tests, experts are trying to discover whether such sewage and refuse is responsible. But in the meantime the local and regional media (perhaps the national media, too, if the beaches are nationally known and – as is very likely – it happens to be the August 'silly season', in which big stories are scarce) will be pressing for explanations of what caused the *E.coli* outbreak.

As the press officer of the local council, you might be tempted to accept an invitation to appear on the regional television news programme that evening to talk about the outbreak and its possible causes. Your employers may be pressing you to appear, because otherwise, while the experts are wrangling, the public will panic, holiday bookings will be cancelled by the hundred, and people thinking of visiting the seaside resort next year will decide not to come after all.

All the same, there is a powerful case for a council spokesman *not* appearing. What could you say that would make the situation better from the resort's point of view?

You could say that no definite evidence has been found to link the poisoning with sewage and refuse found on local beaches. 'Oh,' the interviewer will certainly say, 'so you accept that sewage and refuse *have* been found on the beaches?'

'Yes,' you reply, 'but there could be other reasons for the outbreak.'

'Like what?'

If you then decline to be specific, pointing out that enquiries are still going on, the interviewer and the public will assume that you are merely trying to distract attention from the council's responsibility. If, on the other hand, you say that it is equally possible that the victims have eaten infected beefburgers, then you have effectively accused the food-stall holders near the beach of possible responsibility – before the true cause has been established. And, anyway, present and future holiday-makers are just as likely to be put off visiting the area if they think locally cooked food may poison them as if they think the sea itself is full of toxins.

Either version would do the resort harm.

Added to which, the food-stall proprietors could well accuse the council of defamation in suggesting their stalls could be responsible before anything was proved.

If you try to blame *anyone* for the outbreak before the cause has been scientifically confirmed, you are almost certain to do more harm than good. You will be thought to be wriggling in order to save yourself, rather than trying to serve the cause of truth. In short, at this stage there is absolutely nothing you could say in a television interview that would make things better, and a lot you could say to make things worse. In such circumstances, it makes better sense to release a short statement to the effect that the council is waiting for the results of scientific enquiries before it comments in any way.

Some viewers will undoubtedly interpret your non-appearance as being, somehow, evidence of guilt. But, if you do appear, you might well be perceived as squirming to evade guilt. There is an old saying that it is sometimes better to stay silent and be thought a fool than to speak and prove it. Substitute 'equivocator' for 'fool', and the maxim applies equally well to a case like this.

But it is highly unlikely that judicious silence can go on for ever.

Once the causes of the outbreak have been established, the imaginary council press officer should be ready to go on all the radio and television programmes he can to publicize what the council is doing to make as sure as humanly possible that no such outbreak of poisoning can happen again. At that point, he would have something positive to say. However, *until* the causes have been established, and there is something positive to say, there is a strong case for saying nothing.

Of course, this is not an ideal solution, especially if it antagonizes the media itself, but it may be the best one available. Usually the media works and thinks from day to day. It has too short a collective memory to hold it against you that you once declined to make yourself available for interview. It is more interested in tomorrow's news – when you may well be able to be more obliging.

15 Avoid 'Off the Record'

Journalists can be irritated, rather than flattered, by information given them on an 'off-the-record' basis. 'Off the record' is ostensibly the most binding way a journalist may be given information. The understanding is that the journalist will not attribute what he is told to anyone, nor use the facts he has been given directly, though he may use them in conditioning the sort of story he writes.

In other words, a journalist about to write a story saying that income tax was to go up might be told 'off the record' that, on the contrary, income tax was to come down, but only on a long-term basis. This would certainly condition the way he wrote his story: he would probably abandon his projected prediction that income tax was going up and instead write a story discounting rumours of a rise in income tax, perhaps hinting that 'some members of the government' were in favour of bringing it down. But he could not imply in any way that he had been given a definite briefing to that effect.

The second most binding condition on which a journalist can be given information is on a non-attributable basis.

In this case, he can use all the facts he has been given *as* facts, but may not reveal their source. He cannot quote anyone directly, though he may resort to some such formula as 'some junior ministers think this or that'.

The least binding is the attributable basis – in which case the journalist can use anything he wants and attribute quotes to anyone who uttered them.

Some journalists like off-the-record briefings. Of course it is flattering and potentially useful to a journalist to be given information that may influence the way he writes the story, even though he cannot quote the off-the-record facts or opinions. In particular, off the record information may prevent a journalist making a fool of himself by writing a story that is simply wrong, but which some official or other source does not want simply and specifically to deny on the record.

However, especially at the level of political prediction, journalists so often write stories that are wrong, without their reputations being damaged, that you need not feel that by failing to stop a journalist writing a story that is wrong or even absurd you are necessarily ruining his professional life.

Giving a journalist information he cannot use is rather like giving an alcoholic a bottle of beer on the strict understanding that he mustn't drink it – you are putting too much trust in human, or at least journalistic, nature. The media lives not by covering up but by disclosure, and a journalist's reputation rests on what he writes, not what he doesn't write.

There was a time when there were many journalists who were trusted by the establishment with all sorts of facts on the understanding they wouldn't use them. This may be regarded as to the credit or discredit of the journalists concerned, but the fact is that there are almost certainly fewer of them now.

The media consists of human beings who, like all human beings, want to extend their power and influence. So they tend to try to make their own rules, based largely on what they can get away with at any given moment. From their point of view, this is a moral course: sitting on facts tends *not* to be one of the rules with which they are comfortable.

So, if a journalist is given some insights on an off-the-record-basis, what tends to happen?

Firstly, he may simply be suspicious of the line he is being fed. If the people feeding him information are not prepared to put their own names to it, how can he be sure that he is not being given a completely wrong steer that just happens to be convenient to the people doing the briefing? If he then uses the 'facts' he has been given as his own, rather than attributing them to someone else, he will be the fall guy if they blow up in his face.

Secondly, though few journalists will simply ignore an off-the-record understanding, they may well be irritated by it – perhaps so irritated that they will seek to do something about it. Given information that they cannot use directly, they may tend to wonder how they can use it indirectly – and then, as the story develops, more and more directly.

One Prime Minister was famous among journalists for saying, 'Eventually everything is on the record'. This is very close to the truth. Consequently an off-the-record briefing involving information that later becomes public knowledge may put the journalist involved in a false position – for which he will not thank you. If he reads a different version of the same facts in another newspaper or hears them on a rival television or radio station, he will feel he has missed a scoop, and see you as the person who bound his hands with the off-the-record stipulation while quite probably opening up on a different basis to his rivals.

From your point of view, talking 'off the record' puts you in the journalist's hands just as much as it puts him in yours. *Never* do it unless you know the journalist and believe him to be a reliable man of his word.

After all, if you are betrayed in an off-the-record understanding, what can you do about it? Very little. You could make the betrayal public, but that would be ill-advised. You would reveal yourself as someone who leaks contentious facts to the media without having the courage to give yourself as the source – so what might you leak next, and about whom? Contacts within your own organization or profession who like to think they can talk to you in confidence will start to wonder what part of the media you will ring up next with tasty, off-the-record morsels about them.

A non-attributable rule is far less complicated and far more satisfactory. The journalist can use as fact everything he is given, provided he doesn't attribute it to the person he is talking to. This is more satisfactory to the journalist – it does not leave him straining to find ways to bring out the facts without flouting his off-the-record undertaking – and it is more satisfactory to you, because it puts you into the journalist's hands to a more limited extent and is harder for him to flout.

A journalist who wants to break an off-the-record undertaking has only to say afterwards, 'Well, I got the information from other sources', and you can't prove he didn't. But if you have a non-attributable rule and the journalist breaks it, that fact is indisputable. You have only to say, 'You promised not to quote me, and you have quoted me', and the journalist cannot wriggle out of it.

The off-the-record process may work on matters of national security, because all parties acknowledge the importance of the subject and respect the rules. On practically all other matters, it can be a gamble and a muddle.

And unless you establish the off-the-record rule *at the outset*, there is no lottery at all – you are *sure* to lose. It is no good waiting until you have made a boob and then saying, 'Could that be off the record?' It won't be. The journalist will feel no obligation to agree. Even if he does agree, he may do it with his fingers crossed, not considering himself bound by such a retrospective bid to take something off the record.

You should make the terms on which you are talking to the journalist quite clear at the outset. You can try saying, 'Do you mind if I tell you *some* things off the record, and I will tell you when we get to them what those things are?' The journalist may agree, but having some parts of an interview on the record and some off it is complicated and usually not very satisfactory. The journalist may become genuinely confused about which parts of the encounter were off the record and which were not – and, if he is unscrupulous, he may pretend to be confused. In such a case you do not have much remedy once the damage is done, partly because someone who tries to speak off the record is not in the strongest moral position and may well be inhibited about making a fuss about it.

In general, it is safest to assume that when you are talking to a journalist you are talking for publication, and not to burden him with material he (you hope) won't use as and how he wants.

16 Will it Go Away?

If you have access to a public relations adviser, it may be good policy to consult him immediately if you have a possible media problem. But sometimes the problem will fade with time, provided you can keep your nerve, and if you can make some sort of judgement about the most likely prognosis you will better be able to assess the best policy for facing it: whether to mount a vigorous defensive public relations exercise or, on the contrary, to avoid making any statements, in the hope that the threatened storm will not happen at all or else soon blow over.

You will be able to remember cases of politicians simply remaining silent (or nearly silent) on touchy matters, and to all intents and purposes getting away with it, their careers more or less intact. The nature of their problem meant that it was likely to recede or go away.

The same principle applies at all levels of the professional and social scale. As a rough rule of thumb, a problem will tend to go away if in essence it doesn't touch any sensitivities in the minds of, on the one hand, the metropolitan media 'elite' or, on the other hand, Middle England.

Usually the media will dig for facts when there are

undisclosed facts to be found, and, so long as those facts remain undisclosed, there is a strong incentive for that digging to go on. If hidden bonuses have been paid to the directors of one of the new private water companies, and you are its public-relations man, you must expect that the media will dig and dig until they bring out the facts. All the ingredients of a problem that will *not* go away are there: 'fat cats' upset both the media elite and Middle England.

In such circumstances, you would need to ask yourself if the bonuses could be hidden until they had, by law, to appear in the company's annual report. The answer might be 'possibly' – unless there was someone in the know in the company whose interest was to damage the directors, such as a trade union representative angry at fat bonuses to directors at a time of small pay increases.

But even if the answer were to be 'possibly', would that automatically dictate silence? No!

When a situation is bound, or almost bound, to be revealed in time, stone-walling may be counter-productive. It may be in your best interest to leak the information yourself, but in terms designed to placate both the media and Middle England. Leaking the story in the most positive and constructive terms that can be devised, and before any sector of the media had a chance to launch an attack based on its own interpretation, could pre-empt an attack.

Were there increased efficiencies in the service provided by the company? Would the directors' bonuses simply bring them into line with the remuneration of directors of other companies? Would remuneration in the form of a bonus (which, unlike a salary increase, could easily be withdrawn in future years) be more acceptable to a suspicious public? If any or all of the above factors applied, a pro-active attitude to the problem might well be the right one to take, and there would be a point in chancing the effects of going public.

But if there is some fact that cannot be glossed over satisfactorily, silence may be the best course – until (and perhaps even after) the media makes a disclosure. Personal scandals, in particular, are best not discussed until they *have* to be, but when they have to be, the defence should be prompt and plausible.

If you are a government minister, or even a council chief executive or trade association chairman, who is having an affair with one or more of the opposite or the same sex at a critical moment in your professional career, the quieter you keep that information the better. Politicians at election time, trade association chairmen during their year of office, council chief executives with over-ambitious deputies – all should keep silent about their private difficulties, in the hope that media interest will wane once the politician is re-elected, the chairman leaves office or the chief executive retires.

But you should be quite clear in your own mind what you will and will not say if any sector of the media does challenge you. Will you make a complete clean breast of it and throw yourself on the mercy and fair-mindedness of your 'employers' and the public or not?

One course would be to say simply that your private life is your own affair, and you will be issuing no further statement. It is a high-risk strategy. You have in effect admitted that there is something in your private life that must be defended against becoming public knowledge. Why should you do that, unless there are skeletons in your cupboard? There is also a further reason for caution: the private skeleton may be a small one, but your mysteriousness will suggest it is a big one.

The times we live in tend to be less concerned with morality than with hypocrisy, or what can be thought of as hypocrisy, and it may seem as if it is a bigger sin to conceal adultery than to commit it. There is more concern about cover-ups than about the nature of what has been covered up, and concealment of any kind makes the public consciousness twitchy – even though, as individuals, members of the public paradoxically reserve the right of concealment about matters concerning themselves and their own business.

All this lessens the possibility that interest in a concealed private flaw will simply blow itself out. However, it does also mean that frankness, or the appearance of frankness, will alleviate the censoriousness and lessen the threat to the 'offender's' career. The important thing is that the information should be presented in such a way that the media and Middle England will feel able to say, 'So what?'

A public figure with an undisclosed skeleton in his cupboard is, if you will excuse a mixed metaphor, a bomb likely to explode at any time. If the skeleton would make him look obnoxious or ridiculous, he may have no choice but to keep his nerve and to hope that his luck will hold and no circumstances arise in which his personal foibles became a stick to beat him with.

Nonetheless, even if he adopts this course, the public figure would do well to work out in advance what he would do and say if he *were* ever approached by the media.

Would he say, 'Any allegations of this kind, and the matter will be put in the hands of my solicitors'? Only if he thinks the sector of the media that approaches him is at least partly bluffing and is not absolutely sure of its facts. Nothing is more calculated to inflame a journalist into pursuing an investigation with zeal than the threat of legal action against him: it suggests that the facts are true, and that the culprit is trying to bully his way out of exposure.

Will he say, 'The facts are true, but it is a private matter. I have done nothing illegal, nor anything I am ashamed of, and it has not affected my ability to do my job'? This may work. It may be politic to assert that he has done nothing that is illegal or affects his capacity to do his job. But using the phrase 'nor anything I am ashamed of' will lose the sympathy of a lot of people who read or hear it. Middle England and its media may well think, 'This man damn well *should* be ashamed of what he has done'.

Or will he say, 'I have no comment to make'? The trouble with this is that it is difficult to keep on saying 'No comment'. If he does so consistently he will look psychotically evasive. If he later changes his tune and does comment, he is seen to be on the retreat. Either way, the media will be encouraged to go on chasing him.

Even in the case of transgressions which many people would regard as grotesque, a simple admission on the lines of, 'I have been foolish, but we are all different' may be enough to prevent the story running for an embarrassing length of time. All that there is to be said has been said, so where can the story go from there? The media and the public are likely to say, 'Next business, please'.

It is always as well to have in your head what you *would* say if challenged, so as to show yourself in the best light possible, but sometimes the moving media caravan will move on so fast that your problem may be superseded before the media gets hold of it. If you represent a health authority that is critically short of hospital beds, that fact may not emerge before the situation has been rectified. If so, the 'story' of the bed shortage will no longer be a story but a mere slice of history – and the media has little taste for that.

In many of the more mundane and less sensational situations there is something to be said for ploughing on in the hope that the 'story' will have become boring history before it can break. Even in more sensational matters, a past sexual affair is less of a story than a current one.

Similarly, a damaging story may not emerge, or may emerge in a half-hearted way, because it is overtaken by other, worse situations or scandals. Cynically, if you are trying to keep the lid on the dangers to the peace process in Northern Ireland, you may be one of the few people to benefit from a Kosovo. The same principle can operate in less cruel and crucial circumstances.

All the same, it is unwise to rely on it. Have your story ready in your own words – even if you hope, with some reason, that events will continue to keep the subject of your or your organization's shortcomings out of the headlines.

17   Press Releases

Who is your press release intended for? Focusing on that question will save you wasting time and help you promote your objectives successfully.

To the cautious soul, composing and sending out a press release – which will not involve personal contact with the media, either in single briefings or a press conference – may seem an ideal solution. But any press release is a message, and any message must take into account the identity and interests of the recipient or recipients as well as those of the sender.

The least winning sort of press release is the one written on the basis of what is on the sender's mind, rather than what is likely to be on the recipient's mind. But what is on the *recipient's* mind is on the whole more likely to be what is on the mind of the public: the reader, listener or viewer.

If, for example, you speak for a health authority which is proud of its detailed work in drawing up plans for reducing waiting times for operations in its hospitals, you may focus on this work at length. In fact, the public is more likely to be interested in results so far, and whether the authority is meeting promises which have been made. If you focus on the recipient of your press release, and what he may well be thinking, you are less likely to waste time and effort producing a press release which repels or bores rather than persuades or attracts.

You may think that the whole point of issuing a press release is that one 'sales pitch', on one sheet of A4 paper, can be sent without further thought to a dozen or more people – a very convenient bit of labour-saving. You would be mistaken. One press release may certainly be sent to a dozen or more people. But some of those people will be potentially more receptive than others to what you are trying to say. You should have those people primarily in mind when you write the release.

Whether you are a charity making a special appeal or a manufacturer who is bringing out a new commercial product, a press release may indeed itself be a way of reaching the maximum number of people with the least effort. But it may also be a tactful way of informing journalists A and B (both of them important contacts) that something new is there to be written about, *without* at the same time excluding, and so antagonizing journalists C, D, E and F, who may be less important contacts but still potentially useful.

It may be easier simply to ring up A and B and tell them what's afoot. It is less trouble to make a telephone call than to prepare and distribute a press release, and, being already on the telephone, you can answer on the spot any questions the journalist may ask. You can also get some idea of whether the journalist is interested or not, and even ask him when he thinks he will be running a piece. However, when they see pieces by A and B already in print, journalists C and D (and perhaps E and F as well) are quite likely to feel that they have been 'scooped'. Since they will not want to be seen as merely following in the footsteps of their rivals, they may not write anything – or nothing friendly.

That is one of the advantages of a press release. Even if the release has been written with A and B specifically in mind, all the recipients start off on an ostensibly equal basis and can phone you and discuss the story on a 'first come, first served' basis. If they then make less of the story than journalists A and B, they will have only themselves or their media organizations to blame, not you.

A press release is best *not* drafted as a complete résumé of the subject, but as a few pointers to those journalists interested enough to follow them up. On the whole, a press release so complete that it doesn't permit of any questions is not a flattering missive to receive. Is the journalist supposed to publish it verbatim, or change a few words in the intro and then use the rest verbatim? Scarcely any journalist in the mainstream media will want to be seen putting his by-line on an almost unedited press release.

But there are other sectors of the media. Some of the free sheets, whose journalistic staffs may be less than superb in both quantity and quality, will publish press releases almost unedited – their accountants consider this a cost-saver – and such publications have a definite use to those who want to put across a message, just because they will use the message uncut and unedited. But there may be an invisible limitation. Everything in such a publication is apt to read too much like an advertisement to be entirely convincing as editorial, and readers who suspect that they are reading guff will not pay it maximum attention.

Ideally a good press release points to all the facts and

arguments in favour of your appeal, argument or product, but it does not labour any of them or recite them in detail. As a result, the whole release fits one sheet of A4 paper – with your name, telephone email and fax numbers at the bottom of it, so that the journalist reading it is led inconspicuously into contacting you.

Every journalist likes to feel that a story is *his*. If a press release encourages him to approach you in an effort to develop one aspect of your basic story so as to make a more detailed story that is better suited to his readers, all well and good. It will make him feel the story is his, and he will fight for it harder in the face of possible scepticism from his news desk or features editor.

On the morning he receives the press release a telephone call to the journalist, gently pointing out an area 'that may be of special interest to you, since I know you take a deeper interest in it than most' may yield profitable results. But such calls will be more profitable once the journalist has seen the basic press release than if you made the approach 'cold'. He will already know the basics, and his mind may already be moving towards developing points he has spotted that may yield him a story which will be different from everyone else's.

Four essentials of a good press release are:

1. That it knows its most important target or targets.
2. That it covers all the main arguments, sales points or new factors, but *not* exhaustively.
3. That it makes it easy to contact you or some other designated person for follow-ups.
4. That the main points can be summarized on one sheet of A4 paper – even if detailed information, such as financial

forecasts, technical specifications of products or policies, descriptions of new schools, hospitals or roads, and so on, follow on subsequent pages. Some free sheets will publish such detailed information virtually verbatim.

If it is not aimed primarily at the free sheets, a good press release for the mainstream (as distinct from technical) media should be a starting point, rather than a finishing point. You should succinctly state all the 'sales points' as baits on page one, probably add more detailed facts on successive pages, and make sure you are fully briefed to go into greater detail when any of the bait is taken.

Remember, too, that, apart from its primary informative function, a press release can be important 'evidence' if there are disputes about the accuracy of a story. Moreover, press releases can be useful within the organization which is issuing them. Copies can be distributed to key staff members, so that they can be aware of the line the organization is taking and what it is prepared to say publicly.

18   Leaks

There are three broad categories of people who covertly leak information to the media.

First, there is the junior whistle-blower who leaks confidential information about the organization which employs him.

Second, there is the sophisticated manipulator, often a politician or businessman, who either leaks facts about his opponents that may damage them and further his own interests, or leaks facts about himself and his intentions that he thinks will pave the way for what he wants to achieve.

The third category is statistically the one most likely to involve you at some time in your life. This is the conscientious person connected with some organization who, perhaps through his connection with a related organization, comes to know facts about that related organization which he sees as against the interests of his own organization, or fundamentally unjust, or both and at last says, 'Enough is enough!' and leaks those facts to the media.

Journalists naturally want to encourage as many leaks of information as possible from any of these sorts of leaker. Such leaks are their lifeblood – but it can be gained at the expense of the lifeblood of the leaker, especially if he is a junior whistle-blower.

Suppose that you have taken it upon yourself as a humble employee in the accountancy department of your organization to leak facts about corruption or maladministration. This will be a game in deadly earnest, and you may be the one who will lose most. As an unofficial leaker quite without any sort of corporate backing, you may already have put yourself past the point of no return. Having told someone in the media a tranche of facts, you may not be able to resist them if they go on to demand a further tranche.

You have put yourself completely in the hands of that part of the media to whom you leaked confidential facts in the first place. They may or may not honour their commitment to keep your name out of it. At a later stage, even if they genuinely wish to protect you, they may find themselves having to choose between revealing your name and breaking the law, which they may not be willing to do.

Before you become a junior whistle-blower, count up to ten once, and then again. There may well be circumstances in which notions of ultimate morality outweigh responsibility to your employers or others to whom you owe a duty of confidentiality, but in the average lifetime you are unlikely to encounter such circumstances.

But if you are a humble part of the accountancy department in which there is corruption or maladministration at higher levels, what *do* you do? You tell your immediate superior or the person who is highest in the hierarchy to whom you could report without stepping out of line; that discharges your obligation. You may then very possibly seek out a job in another firm.

If the situation blows up later, you can take the oath in court and say that you reported your suspicions to your immediate or higher superior in the organization, and that you left because no action seemed to have been taken. This will counter any suspicion that you left because you yourself were somehow connected with the corruption or maladministration. To resort to metaphor, it is not your job as a humble foot soldier to cleanse the Officers' Mess of wrongdoing, except through the recognized channels. A self-important failure to realize this may well blight your career more than it blights the careers of the wrongdoers.

The interests of morality in the abstract and of the public may well have been served by your unauthorized leak (though they might have been served by other, less dangerous, means). But we are now looking at it from *your* point of view, as if we were your best friend, your solicitor or your mother, whose main concern was for you rather than for the public good. Any of these people would point out that being known as a whistle-blower could cripple your career and your life. Even potential employers with nothing to hide (if there are any) would ask themselves what would happen if there *were* difficulties; would you soon be on the telephone to a tabloid newspaper or a television programme, telling them everything?

If any tabloid newspaper or television programme tries to argue that you have a moral obligation to blow the whistle, you are entitled to ask if their own employees have a similar obligation to make the company's sensitive affairs public.

So much for the junior whistle-blower – who may well, with the benefit of hindsight, come to the conclusion that he was motivated by vanity or spite as much as morality.

Let us look at the sophisticate who leaks as part of a game of leak and counter-leak to serve his own interests. Such leaking can be beneficial.

Suppose that a party-within-a-party has planned some extremist tactics at a 'secret' meeting. If you are someone less extreme who attended that meeting and are prepared to leak all that happened at it, the result may be to let a lot of air out of the extremists' tyres. At this level, you leak because the nasties usually value secrecy, and you are not a company servant, with obligations to that company, but an equal player in a political game. It is easily arguable that your loyalty is to your own political beliefs, for which your constituents elected you, rather than to any group or sub-group.

The danger facing such leakers is that they may be clever-clever, rather than clever. They tend to be people who think that by judicious leaking of information or misinformation they can manipulate the news, and in the end such manipulators usually meet the fate that tends to befall all those who imagine they can reshape reality to suit themselves. Pride comes before a fall. They come to grief because they cannot see that, once you depart from reality, just one collision with it that you cannot 'fix' will sink you, robbing you of your reputation and possibly your job. Manipulative leakers can emerge as lucky fantasists rather than masters of *realpolitik*. If you are a comparative inno-cent wondering whether to leak, they are not ideal role models.

Journalists themselves naturally don't want the leak and counter-leak game at this level exposed (leaks are too important to their trade, the source of much genuine infor-mation as well as misinformation), so high-level leakers may well sup for a while at the top table. But, even at this level of manipulative leaking, their best friends, solicitors or mothers might well ask them if they have considered all the risks.

Which brings us to the third category of leaker: the one you are most likely to be. This is the leaker who has some corporate backing or justification for what he does and leaks essentially because this is the only way to correct an injustice. His actions can be regarded as legitimate leaking.

Suppose that you are a member of a trust running a local theatre. That trust includes members of the local council (who make up the majority) and other local bodies plus local businessmen and professionals, and you are one of the professionals. The theatre is funded mainly, though not entirely, by the council. Like most such undertakings, it leads a precarious, hand-to-mouth existence, and lately its debts have increased.

You learn through a confidential document from the council that at the end of the current financial year it proposes to stop its subsidy to the theatre completely. (Fed up with putting money into what it regards as a minority interest, it obviously hopes that the winding up of the theatre can be a *fait accompli* before any opposition can be mounted.) The proceedings of the trust generally are confidential, and the trust (dominated by the council members) has voted that the council document remain confidential and not be revealed to the press.

You have formed the view, over a long period of time, that the council are philistines who are trying to do away with the theatre by stealth, and you see the latest manoeuvre as yet another example of its wrecking tactics. What should you do?

If you take the 'proper' view, you are bound by the confidentiality imposed on you as a member of the trust. So you do nothing, and a few months later, when the council reveals its withdrawal of subsidy, it is too late to make other arrangements to save the theatre.

If you take the view that you will honourably resign from the trust and then reveal the council plans, you lose in two ways. You cease to be a member of the trust – in which capacity you could have been of continuing use to those wanting to save the theatre – and yet you will almost certainly still be held to have breached the confidentiality of the trust, albeit retrospectively.

In such circumstances what you should almost certainly do is to become a member of the third group of leakers.

You may simply send a photocopy of all the revealing documents, anonymously, to a local journalist and let him check them out – which he surely will do if he is competent. In some ways this would be the safest course, since you have not revealed yourself at all. But you have left the photocopies as possible evidence against you. And if in some way the leak is ever traced to you, then you will cut a not altogether attractive figure – eager to wound but afraid to strike. It will almost certainly be better if you speak to the journalist on a non-attributable basis, explaining why you are breaching confidentiality, but not necessarily actually passing on any documents.

Hundreds of undesirable moves or situations in the public sector are frustrated by such leaking tactics. As a member of some committee connected with a hospital, you may know of a lethally incompetent surgeon. Naturally the hospital does not want a scandal, but you do not want more unnecessary deaths at the surgeon's hands. If you leak some facts about past deaths at his hands to the media, that immediately creates a situation in which the facts must be faced and answered. You will have brought matters to a head. In such a case, you will tell yourself without compunction that saving lives is more important than any rules of confidentiality.

You may be a member of a parent-teacher association which knows of extensive bullying going on at a particular school. The school, which does not want the facts to leak out to the media, promises to correct the situation – but, after a while, it is obvious that there is still no improvement. Do you go on doing nothing, or do you go to a journalist you trust – perhaps one specializing in educational matters – and tell him, non-attributably, what is happening at the school? Do you then go on to keep him informed of progress (which you could not do if you resigned your membership of the parent-teacher association)?

If, as a member of one public body, you receive a letter from another, you would normally regard that letter and your answer as confidential. But lots of such letters and the answers are leaked when the recipients feel that the public's right to know about some organization's questionable tactics is more important than preserving confidentiality. It boils down to deciding which is more moral: to honour confidentiality or to reveal undesirable machinations. And the correct choice in one set of circumstances may not be correct in another set of circumstances.

If you become involved in any sort of civic or other public affairs, if you join any committee, ruling or monitoring body, you may reach a point where you regard leaking as the best or only means of stopping a wrong. Should you leak? There is a very rough and ready yardstick.

If, despite your attempt to keep your own name out of it, you were to be identified as the leaker, would you cut a positive or a negative figure? Would you have a solid body of approval behind you, or would you be effectively a loner whose motives were neither understood nor respected? Answering that question should enable you to judge whether your motives for leaking are sound or suspect – and whether the outcome of the leak would be judged as essentially constructive or as destructive.

In short, you might consider leaking if:

1. Essential facts could not be brought out in any other way, and you are prepared for possible personal consequences.
2. People in your own organization are doing things against that organization's interest, and you have the status ultimately to defend the leak as part of your responsibility to that organization if you are ever revealed as the leaker.
3. The material leaked is something that some or all parties would like revealed, though they may hesitate because they do not want to be *seen* to reveal it.

You should err on the side of caution if:

1. Your leak is, or could be represented as, based on personal dissatisfaction or spite, rather than concern for the public good.
2. The medium to which you leak might have a vested interest in discrediting you.
3. *Any* party in the affair might have a vested interest in discrediting you.

4. There is no power broker who would have a balancing
   vested interest in supporting you if your involvement
   was exposed.

19   Regular Contacts

Having regular rather than passing contacts with a journalist can be rewarding. He will tend to pay more attention to what you say because you are a known quantity to him: you have never knowingly misled him or lied to him, so when the odds get greater he may still trust what you say, or at least trust in the importance of what you say. And you will tend to trust him more, because you know that if you ask him not to quote you as saying something, but to put it in indirect speech (or do anything else which does not actively flout his journalist's code), he will do it.

If both of you value your regular contact, you will both seek to preserve the relationship. But regular contact with journalists is easier and more profitable if you accept that the process has its own rules.

The first is not to let intimacy blind you to the fact that a journalist is always a journalist, just as a policeman is always a policeman. It is unfair to expect the policeman who is your next-door neighbour to ignore an offence because you are the perpetrator. It is similarly unfair to expect a journalist to ignore a story because you have regular contact with him and the story would embarrass you.

The second is not to be too swayed in any respect by the

fact that you like the journalist personally, especially if your favourable impression has not been tested by experience. If you were asked what sort of man he was and replied, 'Oh very nice', it would probably indicate that you had not weighed him up sufficiently. It has been truly said that one should never blame other people for one's own faulty estimate of them. This applies in the cultivation of regular contacts with national, regional and local journalists as much as in other matters.

Keep *yourself* out of your calculations at this stage. The question is not so much whether *you* like him or not, as what sort of man he is. What do other people who have encountered him professionally say about him? Does he use shorthand, and, if so, is it accurate? Has he ever misquoted anybody? (If he has, you might suggest a tape recorder.) Has he ever broken an agreement about a conversation being non-attributable or off the record?

Questions about his private character and interests are also legitimate. Does he drink heavily? If so, does he do it while working, and with what result? Does he have political or religious views, and, if so, have these influenced what he writes? Does he have any other sort of views, and, if so, do these influence what he writes?

If told about these questions, a journalist would be amused rather than angry, surprised rather than resentful. Almost all journalists regard themselves as writing without fear or favour (though their opinions may rarely differ for long from those of their proprietors) and are surprised if accused of prejudice. Like other people, they can no more sense their own prejudices than they can taste their own saliva.

Certainly provincial reporters dealing on a daily basis

with contacts they will meet again try to write with as little fear or favour as possible, while the 'slant' of journalists on national newspapers when dealing with political or social issues can be predictable. So, if you are regularly presenting stories about useful contributions being made to society by black people, it is unlikely that you would make a journalist from a right-wing tabloid newspaper a regular contact. If you were regularly presenting stories about drug-taking among racial minorities, he might be your top priority.

Perhaps you will *have* to deal with a particular journalist, even though you don't trust him, because he is a specialist in your own field and his organization is one you cannot afford to ignore? In that case you should try not to let your feelings towards him show, but to be on your guard when encountering his danger areas.

Is he prone to report things in highly dramatized terms, so that he may write about your 'defiance' of some regulatory organization when all you have said is that you cannot have the statistics it has demanded ready in the time it has allowed? If he has this habit of hyping everything – and it is not an uncommon one in times of cut-throat competition in the media – you should try to anticipate what the results might be in the particular circumstances.

You could, for instance, tell him: 'We are specifically not defying the regulators. It is merely that we will find it difficult to supply the statistics they want within the three months they have allowed us.' If, after that, he goes on to report that you are defying the regulators, you can point out that you specifically denied you were doing anything of the kind, and seek an apology. If that journalist is going to have regular contact with you, he will know that he will have to mend his ways if he wants future contact to be profitable from his point of view.

But do not assume that every departure from the truth in the report is caused by deliberate mendacity. Newspaper stories are often rewritten in the office long after the reporter has filed, and the appearance of the reporter's by-line on a story does not mean that he personally is responsible for every word of it. A few mistakes may have been introduced by the news desk, and a few more by the sub-editors to whom the story has been passed.

If you protest at a report bearing the by-line of a regular contact, be especially careful not to assume he is responsible because his name appears at the top of it. In particular, do not ring up the reporter and tell him he is an idiot who should know better. He has probably spent that morning telling the news desk and the sub-editors that they have dropped him in deep trouble, and he does not want or need further aggravation from you. However, if you courteously sympathize with his plight and ask for a correction which does not blame him personally, you may well find that he will become your biggest ally in helping to see that you get it.

When you have regular contact with a journalist, it is a relationship worth nurturing and guarding. It may have its ups and downs, but overall it is better to deal with a known journalist than an unknown one.

20 TV, Radio and Print Differences

Television, radio and print publications dictate different styles of response to the media and, perhaps, a difference in the type of person acting as spokesman.

Television is a performance medium. What is required is primarily a performance: the material may be third-rate, but a born performer may get away with it. Silly and shallow people can patently be very good at television, while clever people with odd faces and a lack of superficial self-assurance can be embarrassingly bad. This is not fair (life seldom is) but it is true.

Are television viewers really so stupid that they cannot see through glibness and superficiality? One shrinks from answering that. Let us temporize by saying that glib and superficial people can get away with defending a weak case better if they fall into either of the two categories television primarily requires: the pretty or the grotesque.

Of course, even if that maxim usually holds good, the performance must be suited to the subject matter of the media encounter. A 'front' person for the Church of England should not be a peroxide blonde with a short skirt, but she might well be a woman – one with an attractive personality, rather than an attractive sexuality.

Nonetheless, it is all too easy to create an immediate effect on television by becoming the woman with the low cleavage or the man with the bouffant hair style. There is no point in revealing your bosom or devising an arresting hair style if the viewers remember the bosom or the hair and forget the facts and arguments you have been trying to put across. The key to surviving a television interviewer is not to come on strong in sexual or personality terms but to have clearly in your mind the points you want to put over, and to get them across in the simplest and most direct fashion you can devise.

The fact that a television interview consists of words with pictures does not mean that the pictures make the words easier to follow, as in a children's book. The reverse may be nearer the truth: the pictures may get in the way, and the visual impression you make may compromise the effectiveness of your responses to questions.

A flower in the jacket buttonhole may compromise you in the eyes of people; who do not like flowers in jacket buttonholes. A skirt well above your knees may make it difficult to concentrate on the points you are making about church unity. In some circumstances the lack of a necktie may look like a two-finger sign to the public, while in others wearing one may suggest pomposity.

In general, it is wise to avoid all extremes of dress and behaviour. They might help you to get noticed as a television *entertainer*, but they may compromise you if you are being questioned by a television journalist. Purge yourself as best you can of obvious vanity and exhibitionism. To be a good television spokesman or to be questioned successfully (from your point of view) on television, it is essential that the viewers *like* you and *trust* you, rather than being besotted or entertained by you.

If you are speaking as it were for the Royal Society for the Protection of Animals or the Royal Society for the Protection of Children, you can afford to have misplaced teeth, untidy hair or rumpled clothes. The viewer can see this as going well with a good cause. It could be argued that it would be a positive advantage, since it may suggest to the viewers that you are a self-forgetful person, wedded to a worthy cause rather than your own vanity.

On the other hand, there is no need to overdo this argument. You should certainly aim to appear worthy, but that does not necessarily mean positively dull; you can compromise with television's underlying need for someone striking without going to extremes. Be as presentable as you like, but take care not to look or sound as if you believe that your presentability is the overriding concern in your life.

If this applies when defending 'worthy' causes, it can also apply when defending more dodgy ones. What if you are an estate agent called upon to defend some of the practices of your calling, and you represent a firm that, instead of charging a commission of one and a half per cent of the house price, has decided to ask two per cent? A local or national reporter on television is likely to ask you unsympathetic questions, so you start one-down instead of one-up. In these circumstances it would be fatal to appear in a Savile Row chalk-stripe suit or a Versace dress. What the situation requires is someone who looks pleasant and trustworthy, can find points in favour of the policy and put them in the shortest possible form – in punchy phrases.

'You pay for what you get – we have established that we are on average twenty per cent faster than the average

118

agent in selling domestic properties. Time is money to both vendors and buyers.' Or, 'Our costs of staying in business – especially the increased staffs necessary to cope with heavy demand – are going up faster than house prices, and we cannot continue to give our high standard of service to the public without a modest increase in commission.'

These sort of sound-bites are what television wants and demands. Statistics are best kept to a minimum. In case you are asked you must certainly know the percentage rise in High Street rents over the past ten years, and so on, but do not feel obliged to quote this in detail unless prompted to do so by the interviewer – or not if the briefest figures are sufficiently and immediately conclusive in making your point.

How does this contrast with radio?

Obviously appearance counts for little, except possibly in marginally influencing the interviewer in your favour. In a non-visual medium there can be no other effect which is detectable by the public.

The essence of effective presentation of a case on radio is to create the aura of a conversation between well-informed people who have a common interest in the subject being discussed. A 'performance' will in general come over badly, sounding exaggerated and stagey. Radio puts the listener in the position of a blind person, and blind people are frequently exceptionally perceptive about what a human voice conveys. A flamboyant performance that might be amusing and convincing on television would almost certainly go down like the proverbial lead balloon on radio.

And print journalism?

Newspapers and magazines primarily require facts,

119

figures and arguments, with punchy quotes kept to a minimum (if they are not, the journalist will begin to feel that he is being bombarded by clever advertising slogans). If you are personally unattractive, speak hesitantly and bumble and fumble, you may irritate the print journalists you face, but, so long as you can give them the facts, figures and arguments they require, they will forgive you.

You, as a spokesman, are not on show: the facts are. Print journalists will normally be patient with you if they feel you are trying to help them by putting them fully in the picture. In fact an air of unworldliness (though not of stupidity) may help convince the journalists you face that you are sincere and reliable. 'Sorry, Charles, I misled you there – I meant sixty per cent, not sixty five per cent' may go down well when talking to a print journalist, especially one you already know. It may suggest that you are an honest fellow who does not have every fact glibly on the tip of his tongue but is being thoughtful and will immediately confess to any error. You are *not* a guy who is trying cleverly to put across a misleading version of events!

An attitude of supercilious glibness, which on television might come over as a good performance, even if not perhaps the most convincing one, is almost certain to alienate print journalists. They need to feel that you are there to help them piece together the significant facts for themselves, not that you are giving them a smoothly deceptive spiel.

For television journalists, performance. For radio journalists, conversation. For print journalists, briefing. Those are your ideal objectives.

Nonetheless, despite these differences among the various media, the basic technique of effective response to journalists remains the same: skating round or avoiding as many negative facts as possible, but showing the maximum of well-thought-out honesty when put on the spot by specific questions.

21 Deceptive Approaches

It is bad enough to face media questioning when you know that this is what you are facing. What if you don't know that the person you are confiding in *is* a journalist?

The general position of media regulating bodies has been that deceptive methods of approach by journalists are justified only if the public interest can be served in no other way. But in recent years the concept of the 'public interest' has veered towards the meaning 'anything of interest to the public' – and this can cover the merely salacious as well as the truly scandalous, the merely titillating as well as something that is a real threat to society. This tendency may or may not be socially desirable, but it is a *fact*, and must be acknowledged and coped with as such.

The first rule of survival, therefore, is: don't be so full of yourself that you are blind and deaf to the possible motives of others. This is a reliable working principle for anybody, but doubly so for anyone who is in the public eye in a line of work which happens to interest the more sensationalist press.

If you are a professor of mathematics at one of the older universities, your private flaws may be of little interest to tabloid newspapers, whose readers will not have heard of you and would not be greatly interested if they had. But if you make your living playing a part in a television soap opera, appearing on quiz shows, modelling microscopic frocks or playing football, you must face the fact that – unless you take and keep vows of temperance, chastity and moderation or abstinence in all enjoyable things – you are in the front line for exposure. The front page is eagerly waiting for you.

But no raincoated journalist is going to say, 'I am from the *Daily Smearer*. Is it true that you are an alcoholic on a bottle of gin a day?' You would soon show him the door. The danger comes from men or women who resort to deception by describing themselves as something other than journalists. According to the testimony of some such operators, they have a formidable array of deceitful measures.

Suppose that a well-known pop star is the suspected alcoholic on a bottle of gin a day, and he periodically attends Alcoholics Anonymous meetings. A frank approach by a journalist is unlikely to get anywhere. Instead a pretty girl reporter (or a pretty boy reporter, if the pop star is of that persuasion) will infiltrate the AA meetings posing as an out-of-control drinker. She will get up and declare that she is drinking a bottle and a half of gin a day and badly needs help. The pop star will immediately be interested (he never reached a bottle and a half a day, but the girl looks quite pretty . . .), and soon they will be sharing 'confidences'.

The reporter has gained two advantages: the pop star has spouted out details of his drinking to the meetings, and then he has given more facts to her on a one-to-one basis while she tells him she has always wanted to be a pop star like him and wants to know how. ('Delightful naïvety', he thinks. 'I might just get lucky with this one . . .')

The morality of such procedures is a matter of opinion, but the fact is that they can exist. So, as soon as anyone takes an interest in you which cannot be *wholly* explained in innocent terms, be on your guard. If a person's presence in any sensitive situation does not ring completely true, withdraw from that situation until the person has been checked out – certainly do not blurt out any personal secrets.

Perhaps, at some stage, consider letting the fact that you are suspicious show, so that the suspect, if she really is practising deceit, knows that she is about to be rumbled. That may persuade her to back off, not wanting trouble with media regulatory bodies.

The psychological problem is this. In the main, show business people and other people in the public eye live by advertising themselves, not by curtailing themselves. And this is a part of their psychology which makes them especially vulnerable to deceitful journalism. A journalist will play on it. Somehow you must recognize this fact and learn how to efface yourself at critical moments.

Being full of yourself can readily put you in danger. In a nightclub, if a twenty-year-old girl with ample and largely uncovered breasts chats you up and encourages you to talk about your favourite topic – yourself – beware. Say to yourself, 'Why is this attractive twenty-year-old bothering herself with a pot-bellied man of forty-five, with a double chin, bad breath and very little hair?' (Of course, in practice such ruthlessly honest self-examination is rare, which is why the press may get stories about you which are to your disadvantage.)

How do you recognize a journalist in disguise? It would be true, though a gospel of perfection, to say: by always being less drunk than he or she is. Every journalist would ideally like to be stone cold sober while you are hopelessly inebriated. So, if the young woman or man who is chatting you up is drinking Coca-Cola while plying you with exotic cocktails, make your excuses and run home to your wife, mother or cat. If there is anything about your life you want hidden, it is safer to be paranoid about all approaches than to be deceived by a journalist in mufti.

And if you have already been deceived? It may pay you to release the information yourself – to a rival medium that you believe would give you more sympathetic treatment – before you can be more sensationally 'exposed'. But don't be bluffed into doing this. Make sure the *Daily Smearer* really *does* have solid information before you blurt it all out to a competitor you think may be more kindly disposed to you. A good lawyer would almost certainly advise you also to use in your version of events the fact that you are being 'persecuted' by a journalist who deceived you by posing as something else.

It may be, of course, that you have no personal secrets you wish to keep hidden, but are merely in the position of having to defend the confidences of others. Being a nurse or hospital doctor is an obvious example: you have to protect the privacy of your patients. You must not tell the *Daily Smearer* that this patient has AIDS, or has tried to commit suicide, and no vigilant journalist would waste his time by waving his press card and asking you. What he might do is to pose as someone who could legitimately receive that information. It is not unknown for a journalist to work his way into a hospital, don a white coat, carry a clipboard and ask the first nurse he sees which ward the pop singer or politician is in – once past that hurdle, he can probably piece together a lot of facts before being ejected. As a hospital doctor, nurse or auxiliary worker, never accept a white coat or clipboard as proof of identity. If in doubt, challenge and raise the alarm if not satisfied.

If they are wise, the administrators of your hospital will have made arrangements for supplying reasonable information to the media. But when dealing with celebrities or other people of interest to the media, always be aware of the possibility of deception by the less scrupulous parts of the media. If you detect such deceits, politely refer the perpetrators to the agreed channels of information.

Remember that usually the media do not actively deceive the celebrity or the man in the street. They merely allow him to deceive *himself* that he is an attractive stud, a bewitching conversationalist, a man on the way up, a man who has already 'arrived', or some sort of long-suffering and wildly interesting victim. If human conceit were abolished, deceit would be less rewarding, and newspapers would be half empty.

As it is, anyone of possible interest to the media is wise to follow as far as possible three simple rules:

1. If you wish to survive, do not believe for one moment that rules that apply to mere mortals won't in the end also apply to you.
2. Don't behave like a prat.
3. And – more difficult, but just as advisable – try not to consort with prats who may drag you down with them.

22   Stitching Up

How do you know whether the journalist who has just arrived is setting out to stitch you up by writing an unfavourable piece about you?

Obvious hostility is, of course, the most obvious sign. Faced with this, you have two choices. The first is to chicken out, explaining as casually as you can, 'If this is going to be a stitch-up piece from the beginning, I really can't spare the time.' In that case, the journalist is likely to use the internet, old cuttings and new interviews with your enemies to write the most hostile piece he can contrive – far worse than if you had sat through an obviously hostile grilling.

It is possibly better tactics, when faced with a journalist obviously prejudiced against you, to say good humouredly: 'Oh, it's going to be one of *those*, is it? What fun! Fire away!' You then answer his questions with good-humoured combativeness, your tongue obviously partly in your cheek.

This time, the journalist may be wondering whether *he* isn't the one being stitched up. If he tries to twist your tongue-in-cheek combativeness into serious stuff, perhaps you are prepared for that and will seek to make him look an ass for not seeing when you were joking? Why aren't you acting worried? Have you discussed this encounter with lawyers who have told you how to handle it? Why can't he rile you? And so on.

What you are seeking to do here is to be like the experienced politician who returns each hostile point like a tennis champion returning a serve from a lesser player so fast that it is unreturnable. For all this, you must be sure about every aspect of your facts, opinions and position.

This approach may have its dangers – principally that the journalist will portray you as an over-the-top tease. However, it is probably no more dangerous than adopting a defensive, hesitant manner throughout a hostile interview (never suggest by your manner that you are on the run).

But hostility may not show – the journalist will realize that this will put you on your guard. The real dangers are more insidious. Persistence in one line of questioning, whether obviously hostile or not, can indicate that the journalist has a preconceived agenda which may or may not suit you.

It is quite possible for you, if you are a businessman, to say, 'Sorry, I hope we can get on to more interesting matters soon – what about our increased profits in the past year?' But if the journalist keeps on coming back to a line of questioning for which you can see no obvious reason or rationale? It does not appear to centre on anything topical, nor to have any obvious significance. What is the importance of your health over the past ten years – the only central point you can see in all sorts of different questions?

Thinking furiously while you continue to answer questions with the utmost good humour, you realize why it *could* matter. This line of questioning could be part of a campaign to suggest that your health is likely to prevent you carrying out your job properly – whether that job is leader of the Lower Wallop Council or President of the Royal Academy.

Try to stand back from the questions far enough to spot any non-obvious connection between them. And if the journalist appears to have something on his mind other than the purported subject of the interview, suspect some sort of trap. In that case, while you continue answering his questions with the best of manners, try to guess where he is heading and make sure he has the least possible chance of getting there.

In the case we have been discussing, judiciously drop remarks about your excellent health, your early-morning bicycle rides through Lower Wallop, your daily swim, your surf-boarding holidays. If you can't truthfully do that, then point out that you have had regular medication since your heart attack, and are thus less (rather than more) likely to have another attack than the average man of your age who, unlike you, may not know about furred arteries.

Do all this with assertive good humour, and you will blunt the force of any attack, *unless* the journalist is determined to take no notice of any favourable words you may utter. In that event, he may produce a piece that will justify an unanswerable complaint to the regulatory body covering whichever branch of the media featured your encounter. One way or the other, the result will be better for you if you can sense the journalist's area of predetermination at the earliest possible moment, so that you may take some sort of remedial action.

But the best sort of remedy is prevention rather than

cure. If a journalist who asks to see you has a reputation for stitching people up, it may be best simply to say that you are not available for interview. Yes, he may take offence. On the other hand, he is probably more used to refusals than the average journalist, so he may not. It may be that he will mellow with time (though don't hold your breath in anticipation), in which case you can relent next time he asks to interview you.

In any case, if the questions you expect to be asked concern the organization or organizations you represent, rather than you personally, and if you rehearse all your answers to the most difficult questions you think he could ask, there is very little to be afraid of, even if the journalist is hostile. His sector of the media will be against you anyway, and the comments you may make will be only a sideshow. What you need to do is decide whether you want to be questioned by that part of the media, irrespective of the person who does the questioning.

If you do decide to go ahead, you can only present your case as fully and as convincingly as you can, and hope that enough of your good points will come across in an otherwise hostile piece of reporting. Those readers, listeners or viewers who are hostile to you will enjoy the hostility, while those who remain open-minded will sense the good points about you and your cause.

Always remember that those journalists who specialize in stitching up every one they speak to (*a*) tend to create sympathy for the person stitched up and (*b*) tend not to have prolonged careers before they are sidelined as embarrassments to their employers' businesses. The more justified complaints are made about the knee-jerk stitcher-up, the more the sidelining process may be precipitated (may be; it is not certain). In general, the best advice is not to complain, but to know better next time.

Have an off-putting secretary taking notes, a PR minder with you, a tape recorder running or decline the interview altogether while making it plain that you are prepared to talk to anyone else.

23 Strictly Informal

Sometimes journalists may ask to see you not because they are after a particular story, but just for 'informal chat', because they are interested in your general area of activity. Such invitations can have their advantages and their dangers. They may help build up friendly contacts in the media who will one day be useful to you. But they may also beguile you into dropping your guard and saying more than you ought to, because you feel the journalist is, in effect, off duty.

Police officers, doctors and journalists are *never* really off duty. They may be technically on holiday or having a day off, but if they encounter certain circumstances – an attempted robbery in the case of the police officer, a man suffering a heart attack in the street in the case of the doctor or an unexpected story that comes to light in an 'only informal' conversation in the case of the journalist – they will instantly be back on duty again. So how should you react to invitations from media people for a 'general chat'?

By way of example, let us suppose that you are the newly-appointed sales manager of a company which makes machine tools and is constantly evolving new ones and the patents that go with them. The company enjoys a lot of esteem in its field, especially for developing new ideas.

As the sales manager of such a company, you are an obvious contact for someone writing for the trade press, or on engineering or exports for a non-specialist newspaper or magazine. When journalist X contacts you, you consult your firm's press officer, if it has one, and she tells you that journalist X is influential in the engineering sector and it would be useful to be on good terms with him. He is not pursuing any story, but would like to meet you. He likes a drink and has suggested that you might have a midday drink with him in a pub which he recommends. The press officer says she sees no reason why you shouldn't meet him.

Press officers are useful professionals, but in similar circumstances you should pay attention to your own judgement as well as theirs. First, should you meet journalist X at all, if he is not pursuing a specific story which could do your firm some good? By all means do, since the more contacts you have in the media at the time when you have something specific to say, the better.

There is no point of principle against meeting the man, but there could be points of practice. It could be that now is not an ideal time for such a 'chat'. If your firm has several ideas in development, and he asks you whether it has any new ideas, how do you answer? If you tell a direct lie and say no, he may remember it against you when you seek publicity for one of those new ideas once it is safely patented and protected from rival firms.

Should you tell him about the new ideas after first swearing him to secrecy until the time is ready to make an announcement? That would not be wise. You do not yet know the journalist, or how reliable his word is. If he leaks the story about one new idea to a different, non-competing sector of the media, and then claims he must proceed with a story because his rivals will now be chasing it up, what would you do, apart from grind your teeth?

You could, more advisedly, say, 'Yes, we have some new ideas, but none I can talk about at the moment.' This would be better than a flat lie or incontinent revelations, but would leave the journalist restive. He might extract a promise from you that you would tell him first when you are ready to talk – but if you kept that promise, you might offend every other competing journalist.

So it could well be that your own judgement tells you not to see the journalist at all at this juncture. Do not tell him that the reason is that there are areas which at present you could not talk about. That will only whet his appetite and make him wonder what those areas could be. If he knows his subject, he may be able to deduce what your firm could be doing at the present moment. So what if he makes a guess and asks you directly whether it is correct? You would have to say, 'No comment' – a phrase which is always irritating to a journalist, suggesting he is being arbitrarily brushed off.

If you are new to your job, there is one ploy you could use to avoid the meeting, one which the journalist could not resent. This is to point out that you are new to the job, have hardly had a chance to get your feet under the table, and therefore think that you could have a much more useful chat with him at a later stage.

He may accept this: after all, he doesn't want to be on bad terms with you either. But if he forces a future appointment out of you, which in your view is still too soon, wait till nearer the time and then postpone the appointment for as long as you can decently suggest.

Let us now assume that there are no sensitive areas on which he could question you, and that you have decided to see journalist X. You are left with the question of suitable time and place.

The fact that journalist X has suggested midday drinks in a pub, rather than lunch, is not too promising. Is he a hardened soak? Does he want to create another drinking buddy, rather than professional contact? It might be advisable to consult the press officer on this point.

You may not want to be put in the position of either having to drink at midday – which may befuddle your afternoon – or risk offending him by sitting there drinking mineral water while he lowers pints of beer or double whiskies. You could counter-suggest lunch at a restaurant, making it clear that you would be delighted to have him as your guest and pick up the tab. He can then drink as much wine as he wants while you take an occasional sip and stay in control.

If there is a local hotel which does afternoon tea, you could suggest he joins you in that, fixing a time as late in the afternoon as he will accept. This will preserve as much of your working day as possible before you embark on what may well be a time-wasting exercise. If it does prove to be a time-wasting exercise – with the journalist appearing to be more interested in the food and drink and what *he* is saying than in your company's activities or in your industry generally – you will take care in future not to make the same mistake twice.

(But during *this* lunch or tea you will, of course, behave

in such a way that journalist X's view of his own importance is enhanced rather than reduced.)

Chatting apparently at random with any sector of the media can be both dangerous and irritating, but at the very least it will tell you something about the journalist concerned, especially if your interviewing technique is as good as his should be. It will also give the journalist the impression that you are prepared to think aloud for his benefit. This is always flattering. It is also a sign that you may be a very useful future contact: one not to be carelessly offended.

24 In the Picture

How can you prevent media photographers making you look grotesque – an idiot, a lecher, a crook, a lunatic or worse?

Guests at public-relations parties celebrating or promoting some commercial product or happening tend to fare especially badly in the colour-magazine sections of newspapers. A glamorous pop singer of a former era has pink patches on her cheeks that look like plastic discs suspended from her nose; the face of a handsome ladies' man appears almost covered by angry red sores; or a bearded male guest, pictured with his mouth open, looks like a carp about to swallow a minnow. A woman seems to be wearing a length of gilt carpet where her hair should be, and another's nose is so elongated by the camera lens that it looks like a length of hosepipe. A pop star gesticulates in such a way that he appears to be about to poke his finger straight in your eye, while a renowned broadcaster's exaggeratedly bloated red nose and droopy eyes suggest he is on at least a bottle of Scotch a day, and a dinner-jacketed man with a row of medals on his chest appears to have a large pillow stuffed inside his shirt at waist level.

And all of them look like incompetently made waxworks.

137

There is a character in Joseph Conrad's great novel *The Secret Agent* referred to as the dynamiter. He is an anarchist dwarf with such contempt for what he regards as the meretricious society of his day that he walks around carrying dynamite which will blow up if he releases his grip on a rubber bulb in his coat pocket – nobody, including the police, dares approach him. Do photographers at these PR events, and their picture editors, have a similar contempt for modern celebrity? (Indeed, do the celebrities share it themselves? Their willingness to be lampooned in this subterranean way otherwise suggests masochism.)

Why do people turn up at such events? Looking at the sort of celebrity mugshots we are talking about makes this a difficult question to answer. The whole effect is as if some more than slightly unhinged, puritanical successor to the dynamiter has put his faith not in dynamite but in the camera lens. Regarding many of today's celebrities as tatty and transitory trash, he has decided to expose them to ridicule and contempt while ostensibly doing nothing of the kind. Indeed he fervently protests about difficulties with flashlights in confined spaces and – in particular – argues that if anyone didn't like their picture being taken, they would surely stay away.

But supposing that in practice you can't stay away? Suppose you think your presence would do something positive for the organization throwing the event? You are not someone who would do anything for publicity, and you do not want to be portrayed as too personally repellant, yet you nevertheless decide that some good purpose will be served if you attended, say, a charity PR social event. Is there anything you can do to minimize the risk of seeming suddenly to have become, at best, a hardened toper or a homicidal maniac?

There is. You can take defensive measures or assertive measures.

First, the defensive measures.

Before you enter the room, not after, wipe all perspiration off your face.

Then you must give a ceaseless performance *all* the time, not just when you spot a camera pointing at you.

Do not stand with your mouth hanging open. If you are speaking, do not mouth your words as though expecting to be lip-read: you will look as if you are trying to catch flies in your mouth. Move your mouth as little as possible, and if you have any misplaced or cracked teeth, do not smile broadly enough to show them.

If you are holding a drink, hold it in a way which suggests that you are neither a ballet dancer nor a nightclub bouncer. One of the best ways to make sure you do not drop your glass when also holding a canapé in the same hand is to run your little finger under the bottom of the glass to support it, but this can look rather spider-like in photographs and should be reconsidered at photo-events.

If you have a 'good' profile and a 'bad' profile, try to stand where it would be difficult for a photographer to approach you on your bad side.

Avoid wearing flat spectacle lenses that may reflect a photographer's flash, showing you with two glaring headlamps where your eyes should be.

If a photographer has his lens pointing at you and you do not wish to be photographed at that moment, look away.

(Do not scratch your head, hoping that your arm will conceal your face. If the photographer's flash captures you like that, the result is unlikely to be flattering.)

If you are prepared to exert yourself in order not to be photographed, but you do not wish to offend the photographers, simply stand well away from people who are more celebrated or photogenic than you are, and so likely to attract photographers. Even if you are a doctor of nuclear-physics, few photographers are likely to bother with you if you stand well away from the members of a pop group. And the few who do bother will know who you are; they may be more sympathetic, and therefore disinclined to take a picture of you bending down to tie your shoelace.

All this is based on the defensive assumption that you wish to *avoid* appearing in the 'rogues' gallery' of the colour magazines.

Of course, you may take the robust and assertive view that, though you do not wish to look grotesque, photographs of you may serve some cause. In that case, reverse the procedure. You *want* to be seen and photographed, so make it easy for the photographers to alight on you and get the best picture they can.

Almost any sartorial eccentricity can be useful in this respect, from flamboyant bow ties and Panama hats worn indoors to white suits worn with red braces.

Far from steering clear of better known celebrities, go up to them and force a handshake on them or engage them in enforced conversation. (But remember that a photograph of you talking while the person you are talking to

140

is visibly falling asleep will not enhance public perception of your conversational powers. Watch for drooping eyelids, on your audience as much as on yourself.)
Above all, make sure that your face is never masked by anything or anyone else when the cameras are about. The safe maxim is: if you can see the camera it can see you.

As to the final results, though, be prepared for the possibility that your own mother may not recognize you from the pictures taken at such PR parties – which, looking at it from one point of view, may be just as well.

You must regard it as the price of visibility in a PR machine that photographers and picture editors may indeed secretly despise 'celebrities' or people who can be inflated into celebrity status by constant photographic exposure – even if they also believe that photographs of them sell newspapers and magazines.

25   Chat Shows

There is one vital rule about appearing on chat shows. Don't appear on one unless there is a stronger reason than vanity for doing so. They can drain you of more than the value they give you, leaving a net personal loss.

Although it is unlikely that you will be asked to appear on one unless you are eminent in some way, and therefore reasonably certain about how to cope, it is by no means impossible. You may have done something that brings you into the news, in which case a radio chat show may try to bring you together with people who have had experience of a similar kind.

That experience may be surviving a natural disaster or an illness. Neither will automatically have prepared you for appearing on chat shows, but neither will put you at much risk if you do appear; you are not expected to be a brilliant talker – you have a specific tale to tell, and the tale itself will suffice. Or you may have appeared for the first time in the list of the country's richest people. In that case, you are probably not short of public-relations advice and may be used to appearing in public, but you may still be putting yourself at risk if you agree to appear. Few rich people have more to do with the media than they can help:

the risks outweigh the possible gain. If your fortune runs into millions and you actually or virtually live in a stockade, why come out of it and flaunt yourself on television so that robbers, kidnappers and blackmailers, or the simply unhinged, can start to have speculative thoughts about you?

Whether you are rich or poor, well-known or unknown, you should decide whether to appear *not* on the basis that you are flattered to be asked. The decision should be made on the basis of whether the appearance will help you make any point or points you wish to put across to the public, or what good your appearance will do for a cause you wish to advance, or what good it will do for you personally.

Obviously if you are in a job where personal publicity is important or central – like acting or writing novels, in which case the exposure may help you get another part or win a literary award – any public appearance can be of value to you. If so, you should grab with both hands every chance to appear. Some self-made entrepreneurs, too, court personal publicity and love appearing on chat shows because it establishes or reinforces their brand image; they tend to be exceptions among the rich. For most people personal publicity is not vitally important to their job, and for them the rule about not appearing except for a clear and specific reason definitely holds.

You should ask yourself whether the radio or television programme which has asked you to appear is likely to be listened to by the sort of people you want to reach.

You should also ask yourself whether the presenter is reasonably serious, or is likely to try to draw you into a game of spilling personal confidences about your love life in order to jack up his viewing or listening figures. If he is a moron, or relies for his appeal on pretending to be one, it may be best to give him a miss unless you are confident that the message you want to put across is succinct enough and simple enough for you to put it across despite him.

Whether the presenter or chairman is sympathetic or not, the rule that you should appear only for a specific reason points to *how* you should approach appearing on a chat show. Such shows may be many things, but one thing they are *not* is chat. What they require is, in essence, a performance.

You must prepare what you want to say, and you must prepare it in so many ways that, whatever questions you are asked, you will have a ready answer that will appear effortless.

Unless you are naturally witty, beware of jokes. If they fail, you will be left looking uncomfortable. In particular, if you are hoping to make apparently 'spontaneous' jokes, you must prepare them very well beforehand and wait for a natural trigger to come up in the programme before you recount one.

Study yourself in front of a mirror. Remove as best you can any habits of speech or movement that a viewer or listener might find irritating with repetition. In particular, avoid throwing in the expression 'you know', which will be detected as highly irritating padding.

Give the impression of being at ease, but do not let the presenter's apparent mood of levity draw you into an embarrassing imitation of it. If you want to remain serious, smile dutifully at his manoeuvre, but remain serious yourself.

You should be clear before you accept the assignment exactly what form it will take. On television, are the guests interviewed separately, sitting in an armchair and then expected to take a side seat on a sofa, so that they can be recalled to continue taking part once the interviews-in-chief are over? If so, do not give the impression that you are interested only in your own performance. Establish as early as possible who your fellow guests will be, and have ready a question or remark tailored to them. Your own message will be reinforced by this, because you will not appear to be an unattractive egomaniac with tunnel vision.

On both radio and television chat shows, it is essential to assert yourself from the start. A famous woman novelist appearing on a French television chat show was urged by her public-relations minder to intervene in the conversation (whether or not she was being addressed by the presenter) within 90 seconds of the start of the programme. She interrupted a French novelist who was outlining the plot of his latest novel by suddenly asking him why all Frenchmen seemed to be obsessed by their mothers. The sparks this generated put her firmly on the map.

Such smash and grab tactics may be extreme, and they carry a high risk (unless you say what you have to say in a pleasant manner, you may be thought merely rude). Nevertheless, if you are going to appear on a chat show at all, there is something to be said for making sure you make a definite impression.

It is even more important to make a favourable impression, so avoid anything that smacks of personal rancour. You should seek to give the impression that, whatever you say, you are saying it only to make a point, not to beat down another human being.

If you have any sort of reputation to maintain, the amount of time and energy that should be given to a chat-show appearance would surprise anyone who merely listens or watches. The chat show is a form of theatre, and, as in any other sort of theatre, improvisation has a value. But that value should not be over-estimated. Paradoxically, preparation is essential to create the necessary impression of spontaneity and ease.

How can you be easy and spontaneous if you are worrying that you may not have enough to say and do not know the best way to say it? You can't be. So rehearse segments of your performance in your head beforehand, leaving room for flexibility once you are facing the presenter or chairman.

Remember that most, though not all, chat shows are recorded and edited. This means that in theory your whole appearance could be edited out, and certainly any of your remarks that do not seem 'relevant' will be edited out. So you must think of ploys that will ensure that as little of your material as possible is edited out.

If you have a number of strong, contentious statements to make, so much the better. Others on the show will probably be invited to comment on these, or comment on them without invitation, and this means that your original remarks cannot be edited out without making those comments incomprehensible.

How can you make it more likely that the comments of others are edited out than your own? One way is to cover the same ground as a previous speaker, only to express it in more vital and interesting terms. The producer who is editing the tape may decide that there is no point in having the same or a similar thing said twice, and it will be *your* contribution that is more likely to survive.

Like all success, success as a chat-show guest has a price. It may lead to an invitation to do it regularly. This will be flattering, but – unless such work (and it is demanding work) – can be regarded as being in the mainstream of your life's activity, resist it. It could lead to you becoming a drained, empty shell with only the mouth still working. Do any names occur to you?

26 Short-fused

There is one sort of person who should never appear on a chat show – who indeed would be well advised to reconsider some of his basic attitudes before facing the media in *any* context. That is the person who is apt to fly off the handle into defensive rudeness.

Imagine this situation. The finances of the Barnbridge Social Club show a big loss for the first time in years, and there have been rumours of possible fraud. Just after the club's fete and just before the publication of its annual accounts a reporter from the regional newspaper visits the club's treasurer, unexpectedly.

REPORTER: Good morning Mr Blank. Thank you for talking to me.

TREASURER: I haven't said I will talk to you yet. What do you want?

REPORTER: I gather that there has been the biggest loss in human memory shown in the accounts of the Barnbridge Social Club, of which you are treasurer. I wondered if [produces notebook] we could talk about that.

TREASURER: I am afraid I cannot possibly talk about that.

Who told you? They had no business to leak details of the annual accounts before they are released to the press.

REPORTER: So it is true, then?

TREASURER: I did not say it was true, and if you imply that I did say that, there will be trouble for you. I want to know who told you.

REPORTER: I'm very sorry, Mr Blank, but you will understand that a journalist cannot be expected to reveal his sources in such a case.

TREASURER: Then a journalist cannot expect to be talked to in such a case.

REPORTER: Can we please take a bit of the heat out of this? I came to you in good faith to check the facts of a story. You, as treasurer, were the obvious person to come to. Is there the biggest loss in living memory in the accounts this year, and if so, why?

TREASURER: If you imply that I am responsible for any deficiencies in the accounts, I will consult my lawyers and if necessary issue an injunction restraining you from publication.

REPORTER: Why all the agitation about this? No one is implying that any specific individual is responsible in any way, and we are certainly not implying dishonesty, or that someone had their hand in the till.

TREASURER: I certainly did not have my hand in the till.

REPORTER: We just want to get at the facts.

TREASURER: The clear implication is that I, as treasurer, must in some way be responsible. I warn you, I shall tell your editor of your behaviour. And if you publish your story, I shall have no option but to . . .

REPORTER: Talking to my editor is your right, but we have definite information that there is a huge loss shown in the accounts, and we are giving you the right to explain the facts.

TREASURER: I could not talk to you in any case until I had got the approval of my management committee. I must ask you to leave my office. I think your behaviour has been reprehensible in the extreme. For years, your paper has not sent a reporter to cover the annual meetings of the Barnbridge Social Club. Now, all of a sudden, when you think there is a hint of scandal, you turn up here to persecute me. I warn you that my solicitors will be watching very carefully indeed anything that you may write. Leave! You are here without an invitation. You are a trespasser. Get out of my office, or I will have you removed by the police!

REPORTER: Yes, Mr Blank, have the police been involved in this matter?

TREASURER: Out!

REPORTER: It is said that the annual fete lost a great deal of money owing to the freak bad weather on that occasion, and that may have caused . . .

TREASURER: Out!

Story next day in the reporter's regional newspaper:

The treasurer of the Barnbridge Social Club claimed yesterday that he 'certainly did not have my hand in the till' after he was questioned about an alleged shortfall in the accounts of the club for the first time in its 90-year history.

Mr Blank denied there was a 'scandal' and neither confirmed nor denied that there was a big loss when approached by this newspaper, and asked our reporter to leave his office when invited to explain the alleged facts.

Mr Blank threatened to have our reporter removed as 'a trespasser' by the police, but declined to say whether the police had been involved in the matter of the alleged short-fall in the accounts.

He also declined to discuss last year's annual fete, which reputedly lost a great deal of money.

A Barnbridge police spokesman said: 'At this moment in time, no circumstances involving the Barnbridge Social Club have been reported to us.'

Asked if this situation was likely to change later, the spokesman said: 'I cannot comment on that.'

What is the moral of this sad little encounter with the media?

It is that if you instantly take up a defensive or hostile position in reply to what could be seen as a valid enquiry, you will give a picture of guilt and may even hand the reporter words of denial which can easily be quoted against you – in this case: 'I certainly did not have my hand in the till.'

No one had remotely suggested that the treasurer had his hand in the till. It was he himself who resorted to this colourful language, when he could quite easily have avoided it even if he were determined to stonewall the enquiry.

But stonewalling was almost certainly the worst tactic that could have been used: it suggests to any vigilant newshawk that the man he is talking to wants to hide something.

Another mistake was becoming personally hostile to the reporter, who merely had his job to do. It was not his fault that his editor had not seen fit to cover previous years'

annual meetings. Newspapers are inevitably more interested in what is wrong than what is right: they are correc-
tives of public and private wrongs.

What the treasurer should have done was to decide – if
necessary (as it was in this case) in the only split second
available to him – whether he should speak or not. If he
decided not to speak, he should have produced a plausible
and non-confrontational reason. Such a reason did emerge
in the middle of the interview – that he would have to
consult the management committee before talking to the
press – and it would have been much better if the treasurer
had simply said 'Sorry, old chap, but I can't talk to the
press without the authority of the management committee'.

The reporter might then have asked, 'How quickly can
you get that authority, Mr Blank?', but the treasurer could
have waffled over this and left the reporter to depart of his
own accord in a rather less suspicious mood. Alternatively,
he could have suggested that the reporter contact the chairman of the management committee, and given him his
name and telephone number. Before the reporter managed
to telephone the chairman, the treasurer would have been
able to telephone to warn him that a reporter was on his
way, and to have his quotes ready.

Or indeed the treasurer could have asked the chairman
to give him the authority to answer any questions, and
then explained the true facts: that the fete did indeed make
a loss, and that all the losses were not yet fully explained
due to administrative error – hence the mix-up. It would be
sorted out by the time the annual report was published.

'No story there for you, I'm afraid, but nice to see you!'

The result would have been a disappointed reporter but

a far more satisfied treasurer, and the best the reporter could have managed, if he wrote a story at all, would have been an intro such as this:

> Mr Blank, treasurer of the Barnbridge Social Club, revealed yesterday that the annual accounts would be late because it had been necessary to compute heavy losses on the annual fete caused by bad weather.

Don't bother to hold the front page!

So, when you are facing the media, don't shoot from the hip, especially when it is not remotely necessary. It is likely to be counterproductive.

27 Just One Point

Before you face a journalist from any medium, refine your thoughts down to one central point you wish to get across – or, at most, two. A proliferation of facts and arguments will leave the reader, viewer or listener hopelessly confused and unconvinced by any of them. The average human mind cannot think easily on several fronts at once.

It is especially important to remember this when facing radio and television journalists. Even for print journalists you should be clear about what your central point is, and use other points to support it rather than compete with it. A number of apparently unconnected points will be too confusing and too much to remember.

Obviously you must seek to give a satisfactory answer to each question as it comes. Whatever the question, you should turn your answer so that it contributes to the one point you wish to establish, without wandering off into byways, however interesting *you* find them.

Suppose that you are the British spokesman for the (imaginary) Japanese Engineering Enterprises factory in the English Midlands. You agree to be interviewed, and the journalist's first question is whether you are not embarrassed to announce a further round of redundancies, since you have announced so many before.

The conversation goes as follows:

SPOKESMAN: When Japanese Engineering Enterprises first set up their factory here twenty years ago, it poured £15 million of its resources into the plant, a very considerable sum in those days. There was then a large pool of unemployment in the area – some ten per cent, considerably higher than the national average at the time.

JOURNALIST: But at the present time . . .

SPOKESMAN: At that time, the British government was approached to see if it would provide cheap finance, but felt unable to do so. No doubt it had its reasons, but this did mean that Japanese Engineering Enterprises had to go to the City for finance at a time of high interest rates. Just paying the interest has made inroads into the organization's balance sheet for years.

JOURNALIST: But when you carried out your last round of redundancies last year – and it was not the first – in which some 700 workers were made redundant, you said that there would be no more redundancies for the foreseeable future.

SPOKESMAN: The background to that round of redundancies was that there had been a number of industrial disputes. May I remind you that the factory was in danger of complete closure at that time, and was probably saved only because the company introduced a system of works consultation then better known in Japan than this country. But even with this system (which has led to a considerable improvement in industrial relations – man hours lost are down from twenty per year to ten), the company was still able only to break even. There was also the fall in demand from the Pacific Basin nations themselves, which came at the same time.

JOURNALIST: But other companies who depend to some extent on the Pacific Basin have managed to survive without imposing redundancies on the scale you have done.

SPOKESMAN: The figure of one thousand two hundred must be seen in context. We in fact took on many workers in the boom months of last year, and some of those will be the ones we are now making redundant.

JOURNALIST: Do you accept any managerial responsibility for what has been happening to your workforce in the past eighteen months?

SPOKESMAN: The major responsibility rests with the British government . .

JOURNALIST: I am afraid our time is up.

What exactly was the spokesman trying to say? Did you pick it up? No, and neither would anyone else – it did not emerge with clarity until there was no more time available. The spokesman ignored one of the first rules for someone in his position: make one point well, not ten badly.

What was the general drift of the spokesman's defence? That if the British government wanted full employment, it should help overseas companies who were helping to provide it. ALL his answers should have been slanted to that basic argument. Instead he went back to square one, recalling the circumstances in which the factory had been set up, then gave a potted history of unemployment in the region, talked about the company having to pay open-market interest rates instead of preferential ones from the

government, and then dealt with the hiring of more workers last year, in an apparent attempt to suggest that, but for
the company, these people would never have been
employed anyway.

No doubt all the points had some validity, but they were
all rammed willy-nilly into the spokesman's replies, and so
none of them was likely to register on the journalist, the
reader, the viewer or the listener.

Some people might argue that although this argument
could hold good for television or radio confrontations with
the media, it does not hold good for statements made to
the print media. It could be said that it is easier for a *reader*
to look back to the previous answer than it is for a viewer
or listener, but it is not an overriding argument. On
balance, even with the print media, it is vital to make one
point well. And if you do not do it for yourself, the journalist is unlikely to be able to do it for you, even if he does
his best not to confuse his readers.

The same applies even if the spokesman himself or his
PR people have prepared a long article for newspaper use.
To be most effective, such an article should be directed
centrally at one point, not two or three.

The only exception that springs to mind is an article
consisting *purely* of reasons why a certain policy – e.g.
providing cheap finance for overseas companies operating
in Britain – should be followed. If the spokesman had
declined to answer questions personally but had prepared
a statement called 'Twenty Reasons Why The Government
Should Step In', that would have been valid. It would not
go against the one-point-only rule, because there would
indeed be only a single basic point: the need for the
government to step in. With his mind firmly on that point

suggested by the spokesman, the reader would be able to absorb as many *supporting* reasons as he liked. He could break off half way through, and still have the central point clear in his mind.

Seek to hammer home one point, rather than providing a host of points that drift by the reader without making any impact.

28 Recognize Defeat

You are the chairman of a football club in England which has just conclusively beaten a football club in Wales. The evening after the match there was a huge party, attended by officers of both clubs, at which drink flowed copiously and football songs were sung with increasing exuberance. At midnight you led, or took part in, the singing of an old song saying what the English were going to do to the Welsh and why (some of it involving a leek), and why England should rule not only Wales but the entire world.

Representatives of the Welsh club are conspicuously not joining in the singing. Some of them ring up newspapers, asking them to send reporters to witness what is going on. The reporters turn up, and, the next day being a dull news day, the result is front-page stories in all the leading national newspapers. These quote Welsh club officers as saying the behaviour of the English club chairman in leading or taking part in the singing of such songs was racist and indefensible, and that you should resign. They also mention that you are known to be a member of the Cross of St George Group, an organization of English nationalists.

Do you:

1 Take off for an undisclosed destination until the scandal dies down.

2 Say that you are glad this incident has happened because it has exposed the need for a strong English patriotic organization. It is time England stopped being bullied by Scotland and Wales, and you stand by the right of any Englishman to sing any songs he likes at a private party.

3 Say that you and other people singing the song were drunk at the time, and express apologies for what you now recognize as a very stupid incident, but one without racial significance.

4 Say that singing the song was purely a joke, sending up old-fashioned attitudes to national pride, and that no serious conclusions can be drawn from the whole incident.

5 Announce that your fate as chairman is in the hands of the club's board, and that you will comply with their wishes.

6 Resign immediately as chairman of your club's board.

Which solution is the best one, or are there better solutions not mentioned? We will look at each of the listed possibilities in turn.

(1) Trying to make yourself invisible is rarely a good idea in such circumstances. In the first place, any enemies you have inside and outside the club (and the chairman of anything at all has enemies – don't deceive yourself about that) will have a clear field to malign you behind your back and make your position less tenable. The one who is absent from any meeting is not infrequently automatically blamed for whatever has gone wrong.

Secondly, you will put those you leave behind in an impossible position. If you have a holiday home in Spain or Jamaica, the secretary of the club is bound to know its telephone number, and if he refuses to give it to journalists he may damage his own long-term relations with them – which could rebound on the club as a whole.

Thirdly, in practice it is difficult to find anywhere where you will certainly not be recognized. You rent an apartment in a Caribbean private club, but one of the other members, a restaurant critic about to be replaced by his newspaper, greets you warmly as an old friend and then phones his office in London to tip them off where you are – hoping thus to endear himself to his cooling employers.

Unless you are prepared to wear a false beard, nose and spectacles – and perhaps not even then (for such aids are themselves conspicuous) – the chances of not being spotted are slim. Some newspapers pay handsomely for news tips (the whereabouts of the compromised club chairman *would* be a lucrative news tip in such circumstances), and shopkeepers, hotel desk clerks and waiters in restaurants tend to be vigilant about (temporarily or permanently) famous faces; some of them will have contacts among local journalists, who in turn will know the telephone numbers of news desks in London. A man on the run is a hot property, whether he has committed a crime or indiscretion or merely wants some privacy.

Fourthly, flight is commonly perceived as a proof of guilt – what innocent person runs away? Immediately a person becomes invisible in his usual haunts, he becomes psychologically one-down in the eyes of the public. Afterwards, when the media do catch up with him, he can try to argue that he was principally fleeing from media persecution. This may win him some sympathy, but not much. If some people can stay and face the media, why can't he?

Flight is rarely a well-judged, or even a possible, solution to such a dilemma.

What about (2), which in essence amounts to not apologizing, not conceding you were wrong, but using the incident to make propaganda for an unpopular cause? Such a stance would be so out of tune with the spirit of the times that it would be both inadvisable and ineffective. That fact is unpalatable but true. Leave moral rights and wrongs out of it. The spirit of the times may be right or wrong, but it *is* the spirit of the times, and racial issues (or what could be seen as racial issues) are highly sensitive. If the chairman of a German football club during World War II had used a similar fracas to suggest that peace should be made with the heroic British, the sentiment would have been so out of tune with the time and place that it would have achieved nothing but the disappearance of the chairman to a concentration camp, torture chamber or execution block.

In the new millennium, trying to make political propaganda out of an incident involving the drunken singing of a dubious song would be making a mistake. This would put practically every club member's back up, because it would imply that he was more interested in political propaganda than in football, and that he was using the club for his own ends rather than the club's.

In the case of (3), attempting to hide behind the explanation that you were drunk at the time would not be reassuring. What sort of club chairman would be drunk in such circumstances? And even if sincere, the apology would seem glib and, in the case of a man known to be a member of an English nationalist organization, suspect as well. Would such a man really apologize with sincerity for actions known to be in line with his views? A sincere apology implies a determination not to perpetrate the same sort of action in future. Since no one would believe this of the particular individual concerned, an apology and an 'I was drunk' plea would irritate rather than soothe.

As for (4), this would be even less believable. The chairman concerned would not be likely to 'send up' the sort of beliefs he was known to share. No, it would be quite obvious that he sang the song because he shared its sentiments, not because he wished to deride them. If he tried such a line of defence, he would be despised by his own supporters as well as by his critics.

Putting your job in the hands of your fellow club directors and letting them decide whether you go or stay might seem superficially attractive (5).

Implicitly, you admit that you have done something questionable, which is a form of apology. But you also imply that it is not so serious that you feel you simply must offer your resignation. You throw yourself on the mercy of the rest of the board, which can be a shrewd and flattering move. If the other directors don't back you, they inevitably give the public the impression that they are ditching you in your hour of need; the only way they can play the whole incident down for the good of the club is *not* to accept your resignation.

But there are arguments against such a course, especially in such an emotionally charged situation as this. In such a case the board might well accept your resignation. If so, not only would your guilt seem to be confirmed, you would also be in a weaker position than if you had simply done more than apologize for the trouble you had caused and let the board sack you if they wished. Someone who is sacked can be in a more powerful position to argue for compensation than someone who resigns 'voluntarily'.

Also, by leaving the decision to the board, you put the other directors in an uncomfortable position. Even if they finally allow you to stay as chairman, they are unlikely to forgive you for this and are going to wish that you had simplified things for them by either resigning or sweating it out. From your point of view, you hand a group of people, some of whom may have secretly disliked you for years, a loaded gun and give them permission to use it.

On top of all that, the public and the media may well see this course of action as weak and craven – not the sort of thing one expects in a football-club chairman. Throwing yourself on other people's mercy is rarely a wise move.

Finally, there is option (6) – simply resigning with an apology for bringing trouble on the club.

It is important to know when your own position is tenable and when it is not. In this case, the position is not tenable – leading the singing of drunken songs that many would consider racist was a mistake from both the sporting and the political points of view.

In such a situation the best way to get the media off your back may be to go quietly and quickly, after which the media will usually lose interest. It is often only blatant clinging to office when that position is untenable that makes for the eventual destruction of a career.

The public's attention span is so fleeting and fickle that, unless the fictional football club chairman has suffered media denigration that lasts weeks or months, he will be free to reinvent himself in a relatively short time, and by and large only a few people will say 'But don't you remember that you once . . . ?' Reputations created and exploded by the media are more volatile than ever. Success is not permanent but neither are the effects of denigration.

You will have realized that the principles we have discussed can be applied to a much broader terrain than the football field. Public figures at all levels and in all spheres have proved that accepting a deserved slap on the wrist and passing on to fresh pastures is a better tactic than trying to pretend that their faults are in fact the fault of the media.

The media, even when crude, coarse and cruel, is essentially merely the intermediary conveying a message to the public. If there is no message, the messenger can't convey it. But if there is a message, and it can't be denied, it is better to accept responsibility than to lead the media a dance, piling lie upon lie in the forlorn hope that you will never be found out. Lots of people, from US Presidents to humbler sinners, have painfully discovered this.

You may not want to admit that you have lost a battle. But there are times when the best strategy may be to admit to losing the battle so that you can go on and win the war.

29 Début

You are the new development manager for a firm producing electronic toys. You have been in your job less than six months, and it is not one that very often involves talking to journalists – they are usually briefed by the sales manager or the public-relations department – so you have never met a journalist before in a professional capacity.

One of the female members of the public-relations staff of your parent organization abroad suggests that you meet a journalist from a trade magazine covering your field.

He wants to talk to you for an article he is writing about general developments in the electronic toy industry. He is the sort of journalist you would like to know and establish a good relationship with. Equally, you are told, it would be very much in his interests to cultivate you: you would be a useful contact and source of general information on your industry as well as specific information about your company's products and thinking.

The public-relations woman suggests that, as an attraction to the journalist, you talk to him over tea at Claridges Hotel in Mayfair (an august establishment you have never visited, and which the journalist may not have visited either). She will be present throughout the interview.

Do you go ahead on this basis?

In view of your own inexperience of such situations, you may in practice find it politic, or indeed inescapable, to go along with everything she suggests. But, even if you accept, it is vital that you monitor the results of the interview very carefully to see what actually happens, so that you can base your response to future approaches from the public-relations woman or the journalist on what happens this time.

So you may agree to the meeting. However, its suggested form poses some questions which have a wider application.

The first concerns the presence of the PR woman from head office. One-to-one interviews (i.e. not press conferences) tend to go better when they *are* one-to-one and do not involve three or more. Especially if part of the purpose of the interview is to establish good *future* relations, the presence of a third party can be inhibiting, particularly one who might be seen as a head-office spy, watching to see how you deal with the journalist and reporting back.

You may end up inhibited and paying too much inhibiting attention to how you are coming over from the *company's* point of view (something your own innate caution should enable you to handle, without the need of witnesses) and not enough to how you are coming across from the point of view of the *journalist* and his needs. And, of course, if you are a self-confident type who prefers to deal with everybody yourself and to learn from your mistakes, the PR woman's presence may make you feel irritated rather than uneasy.

All the same, there *are* circumstances in which her presence could be an asset. Two immediately suggest themselves. One is when, as here, you are making your début. You are likely to feel out of your own element when facing a journalist, and her presence will give you moral support. The second is if you are asked a question on a subject which is highly sensitive within the company; then you can turn to the public-relations woman and either get her advice or create enough of a diversion to give yourself time to think. Her presence could provide insurance in this case: either she could spontaneously cut in on a sensitive question (thus possibly alerting the journalist that it *was* sensitive, but spreading any blame for the finished article), or you might choose to 'consult' her to check 'a few facts'. If you are new to your job, this would not necessarily make the journalist think you had an incompetently slack grip on your brief.

The other question-mark over the public-relations woman's arrangements for the meeting concerns not what is there but what isn't there. Especially if you are making your début, you need to know some other things beforehand.

On what terms is the meeting to be held? Is everything you say to be attributable to you? Is it non-attributable to you personally but can be stated as the company's position or point of view? This may be more dangerous for you personally, if you make a maladroit answer, than if the gaffe were attributed to you personally, because the company will be angry at being corporately misrepresented.

Is it off-the-record, meaning that facts can be used only as a means of understanding other matters of company policy that may occur from time to time? This arrangement is to be avoided, especially when dealing with journalists you do not already know. From your point of view, the journalist may quote facts in such a careless way that they can be detected as coming from you. From his point of view, it may be irritating to be plied with lots of facts he feels he cannot use without breaching an agreement.

Another question-mark is over the time allotted to the interview, which has not been established. Most media interviews, if they are going at all well, tend to over-run the allotted time; but an allotted time should be agreed, because if the interview is going badly, and you judge that it cannot be retrieved, it will enable you to terminate it without being obviously offensive or evasive. A look at your watch and an, 'I'm afraid our time is up. I must go now,' is all that will be required. If, on the other hand, the interview is going well and you allow it to over-run, the journalist will be flattered that you found the interview so stimulating that you have given him extra time.

Not knowing when you are expected to end the interview can be embarrassing. You will fear either that the journalist thinks you are rambling if you allow the interview to go on, or that he thinks you hostile if you end it too quickly. A set time for the interview will be helpful.

Now, let us suppose that you, as development manager for the electronic toy firm, go ahead with the interview at Claridges just as the public-relations woman has suggested. A tray with a teapot and cups and saucers will arrive, with sandwiches and scones coming somewhat later. Who pours the tea? Everyone sits around looking embarrassed and no one does anything.

Wrong!

The journalist could probably do with his cup of tea and, if he is inexperienced, may be reluctant to start asking questions until the civilities have been observed. You must decide who *you* want to pour the tea.

Do you want to say to the journalist, in effect, 'This is an informal meeting with a media contact I value, and I will pour your tea for you personally?' Or do you want to say, in effect, 'We are both on equal ground and terms here, having our tea poured for us by my public-relations adviser?' It is probably safer at such a début interview to have the PR woman pour the tea, especially if you are too nervous to have a very steady hand. And if you are facing a journalist's questions, the last thing you want to be bothered with is keeping an eye on his cup to see whether it is empty.

There is a counter-argument. Say you encounter a question that you would like time to think about – as well as needing a chance to end eye contact, so that the nervous look in your eyes is not visible. Then you might well find it useful to pour the tea and hand him the sandwich dish yourself.

Fortunately, there is a compromise solution that gives you the best of both worlds. You can ask the public-relations woman beforehand if she would mind seeing that cups and plates are not empty, but warn her that if you need to gather your thoughts and break off eye contact with the journalist, you may yourself say, 'Would you like some more tea?' and pour it, or pass the sandwich dish.

At all events, make sure you have made *some* arrangement beforehand. You might think such matters are trivial, but you would be wrong. They can help to foster the right or the wrong atmosphere.

Suppose you have made no previous tea-pouring arrangements, and the interview starts on the right note

and proceeds fluidly. Indeed you are doing so much talking that you hardly have the chance to drink any tea or
taste the sandwiches and scones that sit neglected on your
plate. After an increasingly mouth-drying hour you come
to the conclusion that, if you do another interview of this
type, you will not take all the responsibility for talking
yourself, but will ask for someone else from your department to be present to field some of the questions.

Wrong!

First, no such decision should be taken purely because
you had no time to consume your tea and scones. The journalist's tea and scones are important, but *your* tea and
scones are of no importance whatever. If the interview is
going well and you are having to talk all the time, all well
and good, even if that means you do not have time for a
single drop of tea in the entire session.

Second, as a general principle, do not import any third
party into interviews you are conducting if you can avoid
it. Bear the entire responsibility (and hardship, if any)
yourself. Your purpose is to dominate the agenda of the
interview without appearing to do so, and you will do this
better if you have no one else to disturb and perhaps divert
your strategic train of thought.

The fact that you are left wiping your brow after any
interview should not lead you to conclude that two
mouths must be better than one. You *should* be wiping your
brow after any interview; it probably means that you have
brought all your material to bear in an effective way. If you
don't feel exhausted and dry-mouthed after an interview,
it may well mean that you have not been trying hard
enough, and the nasty perspiration will come only when
you read the published interview.

It is a brutal fact that your personal feelings when encountering the media in any form do not matter tuppence. The interview as it actually appears is what matters. Better to accept that on your début, when the stakes may be modest, than to learn it later, when the stakes may have been raised considerably.

30 Once Bitten . . .

How do you react when, in your view, you have been let down by a media person?

Suppose you are a high-flying career woman and are approached by a woman newspaper journalist who would like to interview you for a series of profiles of female high-fliers she is writing. You are delighted and flattered. You would like to take part. You see it as a means of advancing your career and also impressing your peers and family.

The woman journalist arrives with her tape recorder. She appears to have a genuine personal interest, as well as a journalistic interest, in women who have 'got on', possibly seeing herself as one such. This makes you warm to her and, you think, her to you.

She lets slip in your friendly preliminary chat over a cup of tea that she herself is from a working-class background. You say that your parents weren't moneyed people, either. She says that she reached national journalism without any help or interest from her parents. You detect no danger signal in this. Why should you? (We will see why later.) In fact it makes you feel closer to the journalist and more trusting. Soon, with the tape running, you are chatting away like old mates.

She goes away, and you hear nothing. Well, you think, that's the way these things happen – a lot of activity, followed by a wait until the feature or features (as distinct from a hard news story) appears.

You are delighted when the first of the series on high-flying women appears and eagerly await the appearance of your own story. When you finally see it occupying the best part of a page, you are delighted.

Then you read it.

It is flattering, but it is also highly embarrassing. This is because the journalist has implied not merely that your parents are working-class – which they would dispute, your father being a teacher – but that they never gave you a bit of encouragement to get on (in fact they were always interested and supportive). Your family are extremely angry about this, asking how you could do this to them.

You are equally angry. What do you do?

The first moral is: always, from the outset, look for signs of bees in bonnets.

The journalist had had a working-class background. To foster an affinity with you, and to make a 'better story', you had to have one, too, although all you had *actually* said was that your people were not well-off – teachers tend not to be.

Perhaps, in order to flatter the journalist or to indicate solidarity with the sisterhood, you had allowed her to see you as being from exactly the same social background. For her part, she had calculated that to portray you as the child of a window cleaner or factory worker made a better story than showing you as the child of a teacher. And the journalist went for the better story rather than the truth.

What do you do? You write her a letter – to which she

replies that she must have misunderstood you on this point during a long conversation. You write a letter to her paper's letters editor and try to put the matter straight by emphasizing that your parents, though indeed far from rich, had always helped and encouraged you to the limit of their means. The letter is published. You fume against the journalist for several weeks afterwards, but eventually put it from your mind.

Some months later the same journalist writes to you again. Her series on high-achieving women was so successful that she is thinking of expanding the subject into a book. Will you co-operate?

Well, will you?

It may not be an easy decision. It will require analytical and dispassionate thought. If you refuse, you may make yourself feel temporarily better for having put her down – at the cost of cutting off your nose to spite your face.

Putting to one side your previous experience of the journalist, ask yourself whether you would like to appear in a book. If the answer is yes, ask yourself whether you would like to appear in a book on this subject. If the answer to this is also yes, ask yourself whether you would like to appear in a book by her.

It may well be that there are a number of journalists and other writers in whose books you would *not* like to appear, but is she one of them? Ignore for the moment your own past grievance. Is her *general* reputation such that you would like to appear in a book by her?

If you have genuinely come to the conclusion that the woman has the morals of an alley cat and the compassion of a boa constrictor, coupled with the journalistic skills of a semi-literate barrow boy, *and* if other people you know and trust (especially those in the media itself) have the same opinion, you might do well to decline, with the greatest of politeness, to be further involved. (You would do it politely because it is never wise to offend a member of the media unnecessarily.)

But if the journalist has generally a good reputation, you will probably decide that you would like to be part of her book notwithstanding past differences. In this case you should not just ring her up, gush that you would love to co-operate by appearing in her book and leave it at that. What if further 'misunderstandings' arose out of your interview or interviews? (Evidently even a tape recorder does not ensure accurate reportage.)

Either on the telephone or in a letter you should refer to the past misunderstanding more in sorrow than in anger, and add that you think it would be helpful if you were to see all references to yourself in typescript at the earliest possible stage. If she will agree to that, you will be glad to co-operate.

Journalists working for newspapers usually dislike showing their stories in advance to people they have talked to. Often, even in the era of the fax machine, this is a question of time rather than principle; daily newspaper journalists in particular often write tight against a deadline, and they are not anxious to discuss points with you while the deadline looms. But – as you can point out to the journalist who previously 'misunderstood' you – there will be plenty of time in the production of a book to let you see material which mentions you. You can even write her a letter saying that you will co-operate on the understanding that these terms are agreed.

It can be impolitic to turn your back completely on a

media person just because he or she has caused you some embarrassment in the past. But you should safeguard yourself in any way you can in future encounters, and the surest way to do this is to have an early sight of any material concerning yourself.

You can even try it on a daily newspaper journalist writing for a deadline that night. If you do, it is tactful to point out that there may be 'technical points' that you may not have made clear but which you could straighten out if you saw the material before publication. It is worth trying, and, if done with an almost apologetic air, it may succeed.

If it fails, accept the refusal with good grace but adopt the utmost caution when talking to the journalist. Make as certain as possible that there is no room for error on crucial points. Spell them out more than once if you think it may be necessary, so that any 'misunderstanding' will be difficult to explain away.

31 Lessons of Emergencies

Most experienced press officers in fields where they may have to encounter emergencies – crashes, fires, floods, water shortages – have a sophisticated technique for dealing with the media when disaster strikes. These techniques may be borrowed and adapted by those people – official and unofficial – who in less dramatic but still critical emergencies find themselves having to talk to the media.

When disasters happen, the media tend to work in three chronological phases, their needs shifting from stage to stage. The same is true, though perhaps in a less clear-cut way, of the media's coverage of any running story.

Initially, there is the first inkling of the emergency, which may be anything from a fire in a dance hall to allegations that an MP has connections with someone charged with financial irregularities. In this early phase, which could be called simply Emergency, journalists will be out simply to establish *what* has happened.

Let us imagine that a new entertainments complex at a seaside resort has caught fire, and that you are the manager of the dance hall or the press officer of the conglomerate that owns the entertainments complex. It has a new type of plastic roof, which was supposed to be fire-proof but which some scientists consider could in intense heat give off toxic fumes (there was dispute at the time of its construction). You know little about such technicalities and are not used to dealing with such emergencies.

The first anyone hears of the fire may be a brief news-agency message based on a tip-off from the emergency services. As the press officer in London, you happen to be on late duty at the time the first calls from journalists start to flood in. It is your first emergency. You probably won't have to deal with it on your own for long – the head of the press office will almost certainly weigh in himself when he hears about it, but in the meantime, whether you are the manager or the junior press officer, it all depends on you.

In the emergency phase journalists will not expect from you anything in the nature of detailed analysis. They will merely want to know what has happened, where, and the extent of the loss of life, if any, and the damage. Through company sources you will prepare a statement of fact which you can read to journalists, and you also give copies of this to any available press office staff, including secretaries, who can deal with enquiries on other telephones. At this stage you will not encumber yourself by becoming bogged down in details you don't need.

Before long, every part of the media will know the basic facts and have their brief stories ready for publication. They will then move on to the second stage, which could be called Examination.

In this far trickier phase, the media will want to know every detail of what happened and why, so as to prepare more complete news stories or background feature articles. They will already have members of the staff heading towards the scene, but if the complex happens to be on, let us say, the Isle of Man, it may well take them some time to get there. In the meantime, they will continue to get all the facts they can from you.

This puts you in a difficult position, because you suddenly remember that there was some controversy about the new roofing material at the time the premises were built. You do *not* at this stage tell callers about your recollection; you keep completely quiet about it until you have checked the background. If someone puts a direct question to you about it, you take the caller's number, say you will check the facts and promise to ring back – a promise you will keep only when you have briefed yourself thoroughly and agreed with your top brass what you are going to say.

You must at this point *anticipate* stage three, which could be called Enquiry – the time when the media are wanting a head or heads to roll – by boning up on the technical facts about the new type of roof. So you ring the architects and get a briefing on its properties, even if it is only so that you know the danger areas of possible questioning.

When you then call journalists back, as promised, do you attempt to answer questions about this yourself, or do you refer them to the architects? There is a case for referring the questioner to the horse's mouth, in this case the architects – but *only* after you have yourself approached them, discussed the matter and come to an agreement. With luck, the argument then will be between the media and the architects rather than the media and your company. Nevertheless, your company has to take the responsibility for appointing the architects and taking the money of the people who used the doomed entertainments complex. Any facts which suggest that your company was careful in the choice of architects, and equally careful in instituting safety measures, should therefore be dug out and used in briefing journalists.

The point about the three phases – Emergency, Examination and Enquiry – is that they are translatable into situations other than physical disasters. They would apply, for instance, in the case of the fictional MP alleged to have connections with someone accused of financial irregularities.

If you are the MP's agent or the party worker who happens to be in the local party's social club when the media rings, you will need reliable basic facts for the Emergency phase, more detailed facts for the Examination stage, and facts which will put your organization in the best possible light for the final Enquiry stage – which almost invariably consists of a search for someone to blame.

Of course, you have to work through each stage chronologically, but from the very first you should bend your mind to *every* stage, so that your answers will be consistent.

In the case of the dance-hall fire, you would not tell journalists engaged on the first phase that the roof was expected to be fire-proof if you will later have to admit that the fire in fact started in the roof; you would lay off the subject of the roof altogether, and brief yourself for possible direct questions. You should keep in mind from the start that the *causes* of the fire could reflect badly on your employers, and begin to prepare the best set of facts about the background to the roof *before* the media start to question you about it.

And, whether you are dealing with a dance-hall fire or an MP with allegedly dodgy connections, you should not be afraid to say politely that you are not yet sure of the facts and will ring back. It is better to look one step behind than to let your employers in for big trouble, and under the cloak of 'emergency', whether affecting a dance hall or an MP, it is possible to be diplomatically ignorant until you can put the best face on things from *your* point of view.

What is true of emergencies is broadly true of any circumstances which may cause you to speak to the media on a continuing basis. Remember the three stages of media coverage. And remember the means of responding to them effectively (from *your* point of view):

1. Be ready as quickly as possible with the basic facts, and be as certain as you can be that they are accurate. If they cannot be checked with one hundred per cent certainty, give them nonetheless – but emphasize that they are the facts to the best of your knowledge at the present time.
2. Obtain detailed and supporting facts as quickly as you can.
3. If you or your organization could possibly be seen as culpable in any way, make sure you have at your fingertips all the facts and arguments in your favour – as well as pertinent answers to all points which are apparently not in your favour, should they be put to you.

32   From a Great Height

You are Brown, the head of a large industrial public company. You have a Jaguar, a Bentley or a Rolls-Royce – or all three. You are constantly being embarrassed by stories in a broadsheet newspaper written by Smith, especially those in which environmental groups are quoted as criticizing your company's alleged tardiness in meeting environmental standards.

Smith is a man half your age. He cycles to his newspaper office every day from the other side of London, wearing shorts and a T-shirt. He seems obsessed by you and what you are and are not doing, and frequently runs stories featuring complaints against your firm and (since you have elected to be a figure very much in the public eye) you.

What do you do?

There are a number of options. One broad category of response could be termed retaliation. This is always problematical.

One form of retaliation would be to seek to discover from Smith's colleagues whether he is a smoker. If he is, you could make a mental note of this and, next time he offers a forum for environmental groups to criticize you for polluting the environment, write a good-humoured letter to his newspaper pointing out that not polluting the environment is not an easy ideal to live up to, as his own pollution of the environment through smoking proves.

But such a move could easily misfire, especially if you yourself enjoy a good cigar. And even if you yourself are a non-smoker, Smith could easily discover how many other members of your board of directors smoke. If he submitted a questionnaire on this point to every member of the board, they would have the stark choice of admitting to smoking or tearing up the questionnaire – which in itself could be made into a story by the persistent Smith.

Still in retaliatory mode, you could employ a private detective to get any dirt he could on Smith. The temptation to do so might be strong, especially if the nature of Smith's sexuality has been questioned (or, on the contrary, proved: to a rather large number of women, including one MP, one notorious titled gadabout, three researchers and two secretaries). But the temptation to dig dirt should be resisted. If it should leak out that you have done so, this would instantly make almost every journalist your enemy, including those who had previously considered themselves enemies of Smith: if you have done this to Smith, will it be their turn next?

Setting out to discredit an individual journalist is almost always a mistake. Even if it works, when the smoke clears you will still be left with your problem, which other journalists may well want to take up; and Smith's friends will certainly remember you and await with interest any story which could be damaging to you.

Retaliation smacks of conspiracy, and conspiracy not infrequently leads to the conspirators falling over their own feet. If you, as head of the company, ask your public relations man or 'corporate affairs director' to get information that can be used against Smith, that director, even if he detests Smith personally, may resent the task and may, if he ever gets on bad terms with you, reveal your controversial request.

So much for the retaliatory approach. Should you, then, try well-concealed bribery? If your company happens to manufacture cars, should you offer Smith the free use of one, telling him jokingly that using a bicycle to cross London may have given him a distorted view of pollution issues? Any such 'greasing of the wheels' is dangerous if used on someone with whom you have been on bad terms. The purest morality might have it that a journalist should not accept 'freebies' from anyone, but in the real world freebies are accepted – although usually on the basis that the journalist can demonstrate that they have bought no special favours from him and are only a pleasantry to cement good relations. Offering to lend Smith a car would therefore seem incredible if you tried to pass it off as a pleasantry – why ever should you be pleasant to a man who had been a thorn in your side?

As a rule of thumb, journalists are not bribeable with money or material possessions in the sense that these will make them write favourably about things they would otherwise have written about adversely. (Of course, some may not be averse to accepting freebies from contacts they would have written up enthusiastically anyway.) Their besetting sin is intellectual, not financial, corruption – like people in other walks of life, some will adopt attitudes or intellectual positions to please their proprietors and enhance their own careers, or because they make them seem fashionable and 'where it's at'. So a crude offer of, in effect, an envelope stuffed with used fivers is unlikely to produce favourable results.

Moreover, in the case we are talking about, Smith's possible personal reactions must be considered. You may find him a nuisance, you may regard him as an eccentric prig, but nothing that you know about him suggests that he is a corrupt humbug who would choose to abandon his bike, even for the best of cars. He may be over-idealistic and very young, but he is probably sharp enough to detect a proffered bribe and ruthless enough to report the offer in print – in which case you are in deeper trouble than when you started.

So, if you decide against retaliation and bribery, what *do* you do?

It may be expedient to put together all the facts you know about Smith (without the aid of possibly embarrassing conspirators) and decide on a more positive approach. You know that Smith is young and idealistic. In that case, he may quite genuinely regard you – with your Rolls-Royce, your villa in Tuscany, your shirts from Jermyn Street and your shoes from Lobb – as some over-fed despoiler of the earth and its wealth. He may not even regard you as a truly human being at all. Why should he? You are a powerful man and a powerful influence. He is young and with that feeling of powerlessness that can affect the young because their time has not yet come and their own brand of ruthlessness is unconscious.

What is the answer? It is to get him – genuinely, and not through threats or bribery – to see you, your company and your activities in a wider perspective.

There are a number of ways to achieve this. One might

be to write a personal letter asking him to a one-to-one lunch, telling him candidly that you feel that knowing a few more facts about your business might help him in reporting on it, and sliding in the admission that you feel rather discouraged that the positive contributions your company has made to the environment are not widely understood. Your letter should imply that common fairness dictates that he accept the invitation.

If he does, the restaurant should not be the boardroom's; that would be too official, and make him feel you were trying to use your own territory to intimidate him. So choose an outside 'no-man's-land' restaurant, but don't go for the most expensive in town; this will just reinforce his view of you as a hog despoiling the earth, as well as suggesting that you are trying to put him down or buy him in some way.

When you are face to face, do not puff yourself up into a caricature, even if you are under attack. Simply be an intelligent human being talking to another human being. It is surprising how many public figures find it difficult to do that; for them, it has become a lost art. In this case, it could be an essential one.

The basic situation is far from unusual. Fundamentally, an older, successful man is facing a much younger critic: a stock relationship. In such circumstances, the younger man feels that he must defend the whole world against you, because you loom so large.

If you talk to him on level terms and in a helpful spirit, as if he were your brother, his perspective may marginally or greatly change. Remember that the young are flattered not so much by praise as by the prospect or illusion of equality. Some of the greatest, if most cynical, newspaper proprietors have turned Young Turks into people prepared to do their bidding simply by giving them the feeling that they have been let in on great events as equal participants.

Of course, this may be a complete illusion. The journalist may be dispensed with when other Young Turks with sharper elbows and fewer principles come along, as they inevitably will. But while a young, 'campaigning' journalist is able to feel he is engaged on important affairs as an equal of his elders, bribes, threats or direct flattery are likely to seem paltry.

So, as you face Smith over the lunch table, you, as the head of a great company, should not take *his* status as a Young Turk lightly or oppose it head on. This would be both tactically and morally wrong. As a journalist, he does have the right to scrutinize the way your vast company operates. And if it is engaged in activities that pose a danger to the environment, inquiring into them is perfectly legitimate.

In fact, if you had a commercial competitor who was profiting from the fact that its environmental practices were *worse* than yours, wouldn't it be in your interests to have its activities exposed? And wouldn't Smith be the ideal media man to expose them? There would be nothing to prevent you, over that lunch, from reporting (on a strictly non-attributable basis) on how that competitor was operating, and how a few more were operating. And, at very least, it might help to ease Smith out of his obsession with you and your affairs.

You should also try to make him realize that the difficulties you face are real, and not merely invented as a PR exercise. You could point out how many people's jobs – including those in the developing countries – depended on your commercial operations, and what would happen to them if their jobs went.

In short, you don't attack Smith head on and tell him that he is a priggish juvenile with his head in the clouds; you put such thoughts aside and seek to show him, as one intelligent man to another, a genuinely rounded picture of the way your company operates. Without ever putting it in so many words, you should aim to help his education and development by showing him that the sort of story he has been writing is *a* truth rather than *the* truth; that there are other considerations that may be fairly borne in mind when writing about your company's activities. At best, he will feel pleased and flattered that you took the time to talk to him on a one-to-one basis, and he will know all about 'the other side' when criticisms of your company crop up in future.

If you aim to build up a better and long-lasting relationship with an individual journalist, do not become threatening, corrupting or too clever by half. If you have good points in your favour, put them to him in circumstances he cannot help but find congenial. Many 'men at the top' actively like 'baring their hearts' (or bits of them) to trusted media people. And, in terms of getting a better press, they do it with some success.

Doing this discreetly is not as difficult as one might imagine since a journalist has a vested interest in not betraying the confidence of a long-term contact. Moreover, men at the top may find it difficult to get genuine opinions and responses from people in their own hierarchy, so the intelligent critic may be the one whose brains they want to pick. At very least, the critic or potential critic is more likely to reveal where the next hammer-blow may be coming from.

In that sense such a relationship starting over a lunch is a trade-off. The journalist gets easier access to you personally when his colleagues are scrambling about trying to get the ear of corporate-affairs directors, communications directors, public-affairs managers, or that shrinking and hard-working humble breed, press officers. Meanwhile, you, as the head of the company (or whatever), possibly get a better press and a sounding board.

33 Links

Whether you are being questioned by a television big shot or the most junior local newspaper reporter, always appear to be answering the specific question asked. Otherwise you may be suspected of being bored by the question, contemptuous of it or – even more likely – evasive.

Say precisely what you intend to say, but do it in such a way that the questioner (and the public) does not notice any disparity between the question asked and the answer given. That is always the yardstick: does the reporter or the public *notice* any disparity? If they don't, you can get away with almost anything.

Listen to how skilfully an experienced politician says his pre-determined piece to a hard-pressing radio interviewer – whatever the actual questions asked. His methods have lessons for far less eminent spokesmen operating at much more basic levels. The most adroit will radiate the greatest friendliness and patience, however hostile the interviewer, compliment him on the sagacity of his question, and then go on to say what he had always intended to say. He does this by finding suitable (or at least undetectable) *link words* to marry the question to their own answer. One of the most useful and simple ways of doing this is to pick out a single word in the interviewer's question and repeat it early in the answer.

Let us assume the questioner asks: 'When are we going to see the rebirth of quality public transport promised in your election manifesto?'

This is how you should *not* respond: 'When your political friends were in power, they did nothing for ten years, so why expect us to do everything in a matter of weeks?'

This reply accuses the interviewer of political bias. Very few journalists who act as interviewers (as distinct from pundits) are politically biased to the extent that they cannot do their jobs effectively, but they are hostile to evasiveness; they are hunting dogs who spot something running, assume it must be a fox, and pursue it. They would be just as tenacious with your political opponents as they are with you.

'They did nothing for ten years', is a political slogan, rather than a considered answer. *Nothing*? This probably means they didn't do enough – in which case, why not say so? It is also a cliché that every incumbent government in living memory has hurled at its predecessor, and every listener probably groans more loudly every time he hears it.

This reply also appears to be evasive. The politician is part of the government now. We don't want to hear about what his predecessors didn't do, we want to hear about what *he* will do and, in particular, what he *has done* to bring about the 'rebirth'.

However, the truth of the situation is that the interviewee has a problem: he has been in power for only a matter of weeks, so he hasn't been able to do much, except lay plans. One solution for this politician would be simply to decline to be interviewed on the grounds that it is too early for him to have much to report on. But such frankness is incompatible with the downside to democracy: that every politician has to be seen all the time to be doing *something*, and has to make himself 'accountable' twenty-four hours a day to explain publicly (or *appear* to explain) what it is that he is doing.

So the politician – or any other variety of less eminent spokesman who can learn from him – *has* to appear before the public. The only thing he can do is to make sure that, while he appears to be answering all questions, he is in fact putting across a pre-determined line.

What does the politician in our example do? He obeys the magic rule that a key word from the question should be repeated early in the answer. It can be done very tenuously. For instance he could say, 'People talk a lot about the rebirth of quality public transport, but we are trying to overcome the effects of ten years of neglect by the previous government . . .'. This answer is better than the first, simply because of the use of the key word 'rebirth'. But the politician goes straight on to complain about the last government, at which point the public – which wants to hear about the present and the future, not about the past – begins to twitch. The transition between the 'bridge' word and the hackneyed theme is too sudden and illogical. A far better response would be: 'We are as determined to bring about the rebirth as we ever were, and to this end I shall shortly be announcing plans for an independent enquiry into methods of funding public transport, which I believe is the key issue in bringing about the rebirth, and defeating the problems which have beset this country for generations.' This *appears* to stay on track of 'rebirth' while in fact promising nothing beyond an enquiry into financing.

Even if the politician had no independent enquiry to announce, he could manage: 'We are as determined to bring about the rebirth as we ever were, but we are determined that whatever we do by way of remedial action will not be merely a flash in the pan: it will be part of a steady progress that the former government never managed – and which, to be perfectly frank with you, no previous government of whatever political complexion has managed.' This is an effective answer because it does not make the use of the connecting word 'rebirth' seem contrived, but does allow the speaker to put the best gloss on the fact that he has nothing definite to promise. He appears to be answering the question, and yet he has sidestepped the essence of the interviewer's question – *when* could we expect to see the rebirth promised in the election manifesto? – without seeming to do so.

There is also another way to conceal side-stepping of the essence of a question, though it is a dangerous one that should be attempted only by those who can do it naturally. This is to cultivate a way of speaking that is habitually so full of tortured syntax, misused verbs and tortured nouns that it is virtually impossible for either interviewer or public to know whether there has been any sleight of hand or not. There have been Prime Ministers, Chancellors of the Exchequer, Foreign Secretaries and other ministers who have done this to perfection. Looking at old newsreels one may wonder why and how they ever got away with it, but the fact is that they did, and some of their successors still do.

But in general, incisiveness in putting across one's own points while *appearing* to follow the questions posed by the journalist is the most reliable course. The public should never notice a dodgy join between question and answer – and it may well not do so, if the word, phrase or even sentence that links the question and the answer is chosen skilfully.

34 Blanketing

Especially if you are being questioned on radio or television, constant interruptions by the journalist can prevent you getting your points across. They can blanket what you are trying to say.

The remedy comes in two parts. First, you must, if required, be prepared to tackle in depth any legitimate area of concern brought forward by the journalist. If you do not, the public will almost certainly side with the journalist. Secondly, if the journalist keeps interrupting and bludgeoning you verbally as you try to explain your case, you must use some reliable techniques for putting him morally in the wrong.

The first point is the most vital. If you hope that sleight of hand or tongue will enable you to evade questions on crucial parts of your case, you are almost certainly deceiving yourself. As a human being yourself, you must realize that other people's priorities are as important to them as yours are to you. If the policy you have to defend touches on other people's concerns, it is perfectly proper for a journalist to ask you questions on behalf of the people who have those concerns – and to go on asking them until he gets a coherent answer.

But the second part, putting the journalist morally in the wrong if he tries to bludgeon you, can be equally demanding.

Imagine you are the spokesman of a firm – let us say a bank – which is proposing to take over another. You appear on radio, national or local, to defend the takeover. The interview proceeds like this:

JOURNALIST: Mr Smith, both the firms concerned have traded satisfactorily for a number of years, and both have shown healthy profits. Why should they be merged when the result may well be fewer branches and a worse service to the customer?

SMITH: It is absolutely untrue to say that the customer will be worse served because . . .

JOURNALIST: But the reason for the proposed takeover is surely to introduce job losses that will be good for the balance sheet and the shareholders, but bad for the people who will be thrown out of work.

SMITH: There is no question of throwing a large number of people out of work because . . .

JOURNALIST: But trade union members at the firm being taken over have already passed a resolution saying that in their opinion the takeover is a major threat to employment in the area, as well as being bad for customers, and that its only reason is to serve the interests of shareholders.

SMITH: That is certainly a point of view that has been expressed, but I will tell you why . . .

JOURNALIST: And a lot of people agree with that conclusion.

SMITH: But may I say that the conclusion is based on false information. For instance . . .

JOURNALIST: In what way false?

We all know what will happen when the spokesman begins to say why the statement is false: the journalist will interrupt him again with another point to his detriment. And poor Smith has not managed to voice a single part of his case.

Smith should have kept his eye more on the ball – the ball being the point he is making at any given time. When he is interrupted, he should not take up the new point the journalist has just introduced, but continue with the point he was making before he was interrupted.

So the first exchange would go as follows:

JOURNALIST: Mr Smith, both the firms concerned have traded satisfactorily for some years and both have shown healthy profits. Why should they be merged when the result may well be fewer branches and a worse service for the customer?

SMITH: It is absolutely untrue to say the customer will be worse off, because . . .

JOURNALIST: But the reason for the takeover . . .

SMITH: May I be allowed to answer your question? Savings by having one branch instead of two in the High Street can and will be passed on to the customer. That must be good for the customer! We have done our research and we have every reason to believe that customers of both the existing banks can be served adequately by having only one branch, at a greatly reduced cost to the management and, therefore, ultimately to the customer.

This time, Smith's point has been adequately made. The journalist responds with his change of tack:

JOURNALIST: But the object of the takeover is surely to introduce job losses that will be good for the balance sheet
and the shareholders, but very bad for the people who
are thrown out of work.

SMITH: There is no question of throwing a large number of
people out of work, because . . .

JOURNALIST: But trade union members of the firm being
taken over have . . .

SMITH: May I come to the trade union members later and,
for now, answer your question? We are familiar with the
numbers, ages and other relevant factors about the
employees of both companies and we are sure that any
redundancies can be introduced by means of natural
wastage, early retirement and voluntary severance on
the best terms we can arrange. There will be no significant forced redundancy.

JOURNALIST: What does 'significant' mean in this context?

Score one to Smith for completing his answer, but take one
off for getting carried away and using a word like 'significant', which has no precise meaning and which can be
made to seem shifty by any journalist.

Smith would have done better to say:

SMITH: . . . There will be the very minimum of enforced
redundancies though naturally I cannot give you
concrete figures at present. What I can tell you is that
there will be full consultation with the unions
concerned. Perhaps you will say that some union
branches have passed resolutions against the proposed
takeover but I think that after the consultations their
fears will largely be set at rest. I gladly concede, with the

benefit of hindsight, that perhaps we should have consulted them sooner, but we are having our first meeting with them in two days' time. The meeting was arranged by ourselves. We do not intend to beat about the bush in this matter.

One can rely on it that the journalist would then put his point about the takeover being good only for the shareholders. It is perhaps the strongest point he has to make and extremely difficult to refute.

SMITH: This takeover will certainly be good for shareholders –
JOURNALIST: So you concede that point? It is difficult to see that it will be good for anyone else.

At this point – if he has not done it sooner – Smith may use a ploy that can be quite effective. That is to remain completely silent after the journalist's overt attack – as if to say, without actually saying it, 'Am I going to be allowed to continue or not? This conversation is pointless unless I can get a few words in.'

Faced with this response, one of the ploys a journalist can use is to try to get the person he is questioning on the run by creating a vacuum in the conversation; that could unnerve the interviewee and make him say *something*, just to fill the vacuum. But in such circumstances, that something could well be ill thought out. Do not fill conversational vacuums just because they are there.

It is a question of clash of wills. You may be too embarrassed simply to sit there saying nothing. Don't be! If anyone is going to be embarrassed, let it be the interviewer.

After all he's supposed to be conducting the proceedings, isn't he? A complete silence can leave an over-forceful media questioner floundering and looking rather silly; it is rather difficult to bully a silent half smile without looking ridiculous.

To take up the threads of the interview, Smith might retort to the attempted blanketing:

SMITH: As I said, it will certainly be good for shareholders – who, let me remind you, may well be pension funds which will provide for your pension and mine. But a more efficiently run business must in due course be good for the public, in terms of the service it receives, and for long-term employment. We are sure that the takeover will not be a victory for anyone at anyone else's expense, it will be a victory for everyone.

If a journalist tries to be clever at your expense, constantly interrupting and trying to throw you off course, the one thing you must *not* do is to become irritable. Think of the interview as a game with arcane rules, and treat it as such. Let the interviewer see, by your half smiles, that you know just what he is up to and regard him as a bit of a naughty boy, rather than an overwhelmingly dangerous presence.

Cut your way out of blanketing with good humour forged in steel. Show anger *only* when it is – and can be seen to be – righteous anger on behalf of a just cause, rather than on behalf of your personal dignity.

35   No Story

If a journalist telephones you or comes to see you in pursuit of a story, it will be extremely difficult to persuade him that there simply isn't one.

If you need to kill or greatly tone down a story based on false or misunderstood information, and which would be unfavourable to you if it appeared, you are more likely to achieve your objective if you know how a journalist's mind works in such circumstances.

He will have latched on to a tip from some source that there is a story and what that story is, and he will be extremely suspicious of any attempt to persuade him that the whole drift of the news tip is mistaken. Remember, a journalist who has to abandon a story can feel rather like a mother deprived of her child; he will consent to the deprivation only reluctantly. And he will almost certainly not consent to it as the result of a direct frontal attack – he will assume that you are engaged in a cover-up. It will require perception and skill, but you must convince him of one of two things. The first is that the facts or interpretation of the 'story' are unsound, and he can abandon it without feeling that he has been professionally bested. (This should be done very gently indeed.) The second is that there may indeed be a story there, but that someone other than you is the villain of it.

Suppose that you are the dealer for a particular make of car in your region, and the motoring correspondent of a regional newspaper asks to see you to discuss the quality of current *used* models you are supplying. When he arrives he tells you that the gearboxes on at least two of the cars you have supplied have failed.

This begins to ring a bell, but you keep a straight face and ask for further details. They soon confirm your suspicions. He produces two letters from a purchaser who claims that the gearbox of the car which he has just bought from you has failed, as did that of the previous one he bought from you: and that in the latest instance you refused to supply him with a new one. The motoring correspondent says that, on the face of it, your refusal and the previous level of failures suggest that there is a fault in the gearbox of the models you have supplied second-hand – one which emerges only with time.

At this point you have to think quickly about exactly how to react. The correspondence is very familiar to you. Indeed it stretches further back than the two cars concerned: after *every* purchase from you (four of them) this customer has returned the car with a damaged gearbox. In your opinion he is such a clumsy driver that it is no wonder he seems to have stripped the gears of every car he has tried to drive. He was obviously a problem customer and eventually you had to send him away empty-handed. Nonetheless, you should be careful before you start talking about him in such a way that the journalist thinks you are smearing your customer in order to vindicate yourself (for that is the way the journalist's mind may work).

The question you should ask is whether *other* customers have made similar complaints. The journalist replies that, yes, some months ago a next-door neighbour of his mentioned trouble with a gearbox on an almost new car. You do not seek to belittle this complaint or the person who made it (especially as he appears to be a neighbour, and possibly a friend, of the journalist); you seek to defuse it instead. You say that you do indeed remember that case – you were able to renovate the gearbox concerned, and that to your knowledge there have been no further complaints. Does he know differently? No, says the journalist, he does not.

You have disposed of that part of the indictment. The way you have done it, by instantly admitting to the second case mentioned, will stand you in good stead: the journalist may now be more prone to believe you when you tell other facts. But, he says, what about the man who appears to have had faulty gearboxes on two cars? Isn't that too much of a coincidence?

You reply, 'It may indeed not be a coincidence.'

This is where anticipating the story a journalist *might* conceivably see will repay the trouble of thinking it out. By now you have got together the letters to and from the gearbox-destroyer, covering his last four cars and their gearboxes. You hand them to the journalist with a more-in-sorrow-than-anger expression on your face. 'It would rather seem as if he and gearboxes are not the best of friends,' you say drily. 'We have tried to accommodate him, but it has been very difficult. I don't think we have anything to apologize for in this instance, do you?'

By this time, the journalist will almost certainly tend to agree with you. He may be still reluctant to abandon his pursuit of a story, but you have conducted yourself in such a way that the story he set out to write – a car-dealer selling a series of dud cars – has been exploded. If he is determined to write a story, it will have to be another one, which does *not* throw mud at your dealership: the story of the driver from hell and his succession of mashed gearboxes.

Whether he does write it or not will be up to him and his editor. You would no doubt be happier if he did not – so as to avoid the slightest risk that some readers would still sympathize with the customer – but at the very least you have managed the maximum possible damage limitation.

The essence of persuading a journalist to drop a story that implicates you in some way is to remain calm, and to try to demolish the case against you in a conversational way that suggests there is no story, rather than a confrontational or evasive way. If, at the same time, you can obliquely suggest another story the journalist could write that does not discredit you, that will appease his desire for a good story and be good insurance from your point of view.

What about non-stories at official and even government levels? Official spokesmen have become accomplished at deterring the pursuit of stories by making the content seem so grey and boring that the journalist eventually tends to lose interest and go after easier prey. But when it is a question of a story that shows the department in a good light, the dramatic phrases flow freely and seductively from the same spokesmen's lips.

All those who face the media may learn from this technique, which consists of drearily deflating all the dramatic 'facts' until the journalist's ballpoint stops writing, or his recorder is switched off, and he profoundly wishes he were somewhere else. A story can only become a story if it interests the public – and if a journalist is bored he will tend to assume that the public will be, too.

In particular, statistics that are potentially damaging can be minimized in this way. Such statistics usually require a dramatic 'trigger' of perception about what they signify to bring them into popular focus, and, through suitably boring presentation, you may be able to see that the journalist does not spot it. Even so, you should provide for the possibility that this ploy may fail, and think out in advance replies to every possible awkward question, so that as much of the drama of the 'trigger' perception can be deflated.

In this way, in this and many other situations, you may not be able to kill a story, but you may be able to draw some of its teeth. Then, even if the media still regard it as a story, it is less likely to be one for the front page or the national or regional television news headlines.

36 Give and Take

Journalists tend to suspect that any trade-offs made with their contacts are an infringement of their professional integrity. It is a sensitive point. The most extreme trade-offs can be dishonest: as it would be if a journalist abandoned a story that would be unfavourable to his contact in return for the proverbial envelope stuffed with used fivers or (more likely) the promise of future exclusive stories.

A journalist of integrity would quite properly resent the suggestion that he can be bribed into serving your interests. All the same, there is a grey area which may legitimately be explored by a journalist's contact, and responded to by the journalist, without ethical compromise.

Always remember that it is a journalist's business to get information, and to get it as early as possible. That fact may sometimes be used to serve your interests.

Let us say you are connected with the stock market, the commodities market, or any other sort of market. Journalists will ring you up day after day to get information about how the market is moving, and the implications, so that they may write their evaluations. This is in effect a service which you provide free, and there is no reason why you should not occasionally try to get a trade-off for this.

Suppose you work in the commodities market, and you hear rumours of a move being made by another organization which could affect the market. Are they any more than rumours? You obviously want to find out, but how can you do so?

You don't want to approach the company concerned because (a) its representatives wouldn't tell you ahead of publication, and (b) you don't want to let them know that you are on to something. You could wait for the evening or morning newspapers, but things might have moved on swiftly before then. You need to know five minutes ago or at least as soon as possible.

So what can you do? You may be able to kill two birds with one stone, by making the journalist who does you a favour feel that you have done him a favour.

Is there a particular journalist to whom you have been useful in providing analytical information? If so, there is no reason why you shouldn't ring him and see if he knows of the rumour, and whether it is correct.

Probably he will not have heard it - your information, though indefinite, is likely to be ahead of his. He will be thankful for what is, to him, a real news tip, which will be a point in your favour. And he can simply ring the company and ask point blank if the story he has heard is true. (He will not reveal the source of the news tip, especially if you ask him not to, because journalists regard it as a matter of principle not to reveal their sensitive sources except with their permission.)

If the story is true, and the company spills the beans,

the journalist will have every reason to ring you back with news of the confirmation, partly as a give-and-take gesture and partly because he wants your comment on it, either attributably or non-attributably. Your rumour is thus confirmed without your having to show your own hand, and without you in any way acting against your own company's interests. Indeed you may be able to act on it, to your company's benefit.

You are happy about all this. The journalist is also happy, because he has obtained a story ahead of anyone else without having to compromise his principles at all: all he has done is follow up a news tip and then ask you to comment on the result.

The same principle and sets of circumstances can apply to many contacts with journalists. Keep firmly in mind always that any action you take should go against neither your own principles nor those of the journalist, whose concern, always, is to get a story.

Suppose you are in theatrical management and hear that a leading actor is to be engaged by the American producer of a film in nine months' time. This is a story that show-business journalists would be glad to have. However, it is not good news for you, for you were hoping (though you hadn't yet mentioned it to him) that the same actor would star in a new stage production of yours at the time.

Plainly, if he is going to Hollywood, he will not be available for your production, and you must approach some other actors double quick. And yet you don't want to make any other approaches directly yourself – one of which might be accepted with alacrity – in case the rumour of the actor's departure for Hollywood was untrue. That would leave you in a very embarrassing position indeed.

Why not simply ring up the preferred actor and ask him what his intentions are? Because, the moment you reveal your hand and your knowledge of his coming lucrative departure, his price is almost bound to go up. And, even if the rumour of his departure is quite untrue, he will know how keen you are to get him.

Once again, you can appeal to what is effectively a journalist's give-and-take. Telephone a journalist you know and put the rumour of the proposed Hollywood departure to him. You need not volunteer your reasons for wanting confirmation (though they may be deduced) although you could be absolutely frank about why you need to know whether the rumour is correct. The latter course would give the journalist a good story one way or the other. If the rumour is true, then the story is that the actor misses the lead in a British stage production because he is off to Hollywood; if it is untrue, then the story is that the actor who missed a Hollywood chance is likely to be the lead in a British stage play.

The fact that you have revealed your interest in the actor may push up his price, but, now it has been established that he is *not* off to Hollywood, his bargaining power may have been reduced, so a compromise deal could still be feasible.

Do not expect a journalist to go against his own professional ethics in giving you such 'unofficial' help. Do not give the impression that you are energetically pumping the journalist for facts, or you will also give him the impression that his integrity is being abused or trifled with. In particular, do not expect him to reveal any personal and unofficial sources he has used in checking out rumours you have put to him – just be content with the fact of whether the rumour is true or false. You have to remember that journalistic ethics are chiefly concerned with the ability to obtain stories. He would regard it as unethical to reveal a confidential source, because it would limit his ability to get sensitive stories in future. So don't expect him to, and steer well clear of any suggestion of such expectation.

Journalists are fairly expert in detecting what a contact is trying to find out about his sources, even if the contact attempts cleverly to disguise it. They are also quick to spot a leading question among a lot of social chit-chat.

Let us suppose that you are a private company's press spokesman, and that you have a good relationship with a journalist covering your company's area of activity. He writes a story about another company's future intentions. You know, and he knows, that there are conflicting points of view within that company about the way the firm should develop. The journalist has quoted no one directly in his story, but has written that 'a source within the company' has indicated it would like to go public and float on the Stock Exchange.

Your own company directors would very much like to know exactly *who* it was who said this – the chairman, who is middle-aged and reputed to be on his way out, or the coming man, the chief executive, who is expected to succeed him. If it was the latter, more weight could be attached to the possibility of a flotation.

You take the journalist out to lunch to discuss 'general

industry conditions' or whatever – an invitation he accepts because he thinks you may have a story for him. Over lunch you do indeed give him some pointers on developments in the industry generally, and even a few on movements within your own company. Then, over coffee, you ask him casually whether he can help you in return. Who was the unnamed source behind his story on the other firm?

You thereby put him in an uncomfortable position. He has just accepted not only your lunch and your brandy (which he may well comfortably disregard as mere social lubrication) but also a few news pointers that may come in useful in future. He will still not want to reveal the identity of his source to you, and he will almost certainly become ice-cold sober and resentful at being asked.

Yet having asked, and been refused, you feel you have to press ahead. You ask how influential on the board of directors would the source be? The journalist, an expert at asking oblique questions himself, resents this turning of the tables and tells you, flatly, that he is sorry, but he simply cannot identify a source who was not anxious to be named.

Ah, you say, that sounds like the chairman, who has always been known as a reticent sort of person. The journalist smiles, rather grimly now, and says still more firmly that he cannot help you.

The point to note is this: if you push it any further, the journalist may, as a matter of professional decision, start to lie to protect his source. He may even tell you that he may do just that, and therefore you should disregard anything that he may say on the subject.

Perhaps, on the other hand, your persistence is such

that the journalist will try to help you obliquely without giving any names. You say your hunch is that it was the chairman speaking; the journalist, desperate for a change of subject, says casually that in life he has often found that it pays to follow your own hunches.

You may be tempted to try to get positive confirmation of that hint. Don't! Accept the oblique help and change the subject. You have got as far as you can without alienating the journalist for good. Already he may be regretting and resenting the fact that he made a seemingly merely philosophical remark, and resenting you for putting him in that situation. If you push him any further don't be surprised if he declines all future lunch invitations – or even, indeed, abruptly terminates the current one.

The concept of give and take between a journalist and a contact breaks down when either side thinks it has been tricked or manoeuvred, or its professional integrity has not been respected. If this happens, it is usually a sign of short-termism. Remember, even the best of journalists may have to cut corners because they are fighting to meet a deadline and time is against them. But they are unlikely to understand the justification that is driving you if you try to cut corners when dealing with them.

It may be unethical for a journalist to reveal his sources, but it certainly is not unethical for a journalist to accept a story from an undisclosed source which is self-interested. If it were, stories would be in much shorter supply and the media would be approaching bankruptcy.

But whatever you do, be as frank as you can be with the journalist. If you play a false or misleading hand in order to manoeuvre him into doing something that will benefit you, you are playing a very dangerous game indeed. It may well be one for which he will not readily forgive you.

37 Disregard Dandruff

Reporter X may or may not be corpulent, heavy-drinking and oafish but to *you* he most certainly isn't – definitely not; don't even think about it!

It is all too easy to allow a poor opinion of the media as a whole, or of certain media personalities, to colour your reaction to media people as individuals when you are face to face with them – especially if they have dandruff, a soiled shirt-collar or trousers showing every sort of crease except immaculate vertical ones.

Try not to let this happen.

This need not be a matter of hypocrisy, merely of not letting unfavourable personal opinions form in your mind unless it is absolutely necessary (which 999 times out of 1,000 it isn't – you are an interviewee, not a genetic engineer).

Simply refuse to let your mind be distracted by any such potentially disruptive thoughts, for that will only hinder the process of getting the best results from your point of view. A journalist who feels scorned can be just as piqued by this, and possibly spiteful, as anyone else would be in that situation.

If you think that, because you take care to hide it, he will not detect your unenthusiastic view of him as a person, you may be underrating his intelligence (although not every journalist is especially intelligent, some are very intelligent indeed). Let us draw an analogy from family life. No doubt you have, or could have, opinions about the members of your spouse's or your partner's family, as he or she could about yours. If you are to survive contact with them, you must simply not let these opinions (often no more than arbitrary prejudices or aesthetic reactions) form in your mind. If you do, but nevertheless behave pleasantly with them, that amounts to conscious hypocrisy, and there is a danger that circumstances will crack it wide open.

Your mental attitude to people in the media, unless it is one of genuine respect and guarded trust acquired over a period of time, should be one of open-mindedness: they are as good as their behaviour towards you on this occasion. Remember the old adage, handsome is as handsome does. If you can do this, something of your attitude will come across to the journalist and will predispose him to give you a 'better press' than if you were either gushing or secretly (you hope) contemptuous.

Being small in stature, bald, bespectacled, physically incapacitated or ugly is not a criminal or moral offence. Neither is having dandruff. It is not even a sign of professional incapacity (though certainly any journalist with dandruff would be well advised to eradicate it if he wants to be unconditionally welcomed by all his contacts).

If you have to deal with people from the media, never admit to yourself that they might have personal attributes which put you off. You must desensitize yourself as much as you can to anything of the sort. (Dandruff? Never observed it! Body odour? No, can't say I have noticed it! Holes in her tights? Really? Smells of beer at ten in the morning? I must have had a cold, never smelt a thing! Bad breath? Ditto.) You will not need to exercise this deliberate mental vagueness in most cases, but you may find it helpful in a few.

Whatever your personal opinion of them may be, people in the media form a vital link between you and the public. Therefore do not form any personal opinion unless it is either absolutely necessary to do so for *functional* reasons (for example because they are personally and professionally dishonest in making up quotes) or safely favourable.

There is no need to pretend what you don't feel. Just remain wishy-washy and see that you don't feel anything superfluous that gets in the way of your dealing with media people effectively. If you are more concerned about your interests than about your personal fastidiousness, the outcome of your dealings with them is likely to be more advantageous to you.

38 Some Final Thoughts

As ever, the basic principles of dealing with journalists remain rooted in satisfactory human contact, but the electronics age has certainly altered many of the practices. At the most basic level, the journalist is frequently not the person on the spot but the person on the telephone.

Telephone calls with a journalist can be easier to deal with than meeting him face to face; you are not under his eagle eyes, you are on your 'home ground' of home or office, and you have the ultimate sanction of ringing off. All the same, elementary precautions should be taken.

Is the person you are talking to a *bona fide* journalist? Make sure you ask and note down his name and that of the media organization he represents.

Is he a freelance? More and more journalists are, though their loyalty to the organization for which they are seeking a story can be looser and more transitory than that of a staff journalist. Anyone can call himself a freelance, but might not be acceptable to any reputable journalistic organization.

If in doubt, when you are telephoned by a journalist you do not know and have never heard of, say that you will ring him back. Then make enquiries before you do so.

Telephone the organization which he says has commissioned him to approach you.

If the journalist is a freelance working 'on spec', as distinct from being commissioned, it may pay you to approach a friendly journalist you *do* know and ask about him. It may also pay you to meet him face to face in the first instance rather than talking to an unknown voice on the telephone or an unknown keyboard operator on the Internet.

At the more complex end of the electronics spectrum, stories you are asked to comment on may have been released via the Internet, which in practice is less well regulated by law (for instance, in matters of libel) than more traditional means of releasing stories.

Some public relations experts argue that the Internet will revolutionize the whole art and craft of dealing with the media. Certainly you or your organization can establish a website which is full of information about you or it, should anyone care to pay attention to it. And you or your organization can email your way into newspaper offices, television studios and political centres of power in a way that was unthinkable only a few years ago.

What notice is taken of all this electronic input is another matter. It is arguable that the Internet will inevitably create a new sort of professional: the rubbish-excluder. (His function will be to supply those who pay him high fees not with more information but with less; he will effectively 'spike' all Internet output of low or non-existent value, so that it does not waste the time of his paymasters.) Do not let technology blind you to the fact that effective communication with the media is still based on the human principles: maximum possible honesty, clarity of thought, promptness of reaction and an instinct for keeping on the right side of genuine human values and public sensibilities. Rubbish does not cease to be rubbish because it arrives over the Internet rather than in a dog-eared press release.

In particular, bear in mind that, because of the comparative lack of regulation of the system, a story on the Internet may be less trustworthy than a story publicized by more traditional methods. If such a story is prejudicial to you or your organization, should you ignore it and hope that it will be either not read or read but ignored? Hardly. Stories that have affected the lives of many, including American politicians, were first circulated on the Internet.

Usually the signal that such a story cannot be ignored is when it is taken up by a newspaper, magazine, radio station or television programme – all of which are legally accountable and cannot be ignored. Nonetheless, even if you decide not to respond to a story on the Internet, you should have a statement prepared in case the pressure on you to say something builds up. It is better to tear a statement up unused than to be caught without one.

Bear in mind that a press statement is not quite the same thing as a press release. A press release is usually written well ahead of publication about a set of circumstances which are predictable; a press statement is usually a reaction to a media story or unexpected set of circumstances. A press release may possibly be highly detailed, but a press statement should say only what *needs* to be said at the time it is made in order to explain a set of circumstances or forestall and offset criticism before a compromising situation develops.

You might think that to dwell on the difference between a press release and a press statement is just nit-picking.

Many public relations practitioners would argue otherwise. They would say that a press statement is essentially a statement of individual or corporate policy or practice. It may be drawn up but never used (e.g., if an anticipated set of circumstances does not materialize), whereas no one in his right mind would draw up a press release if he did not intend to send it out. But a press release may *contain* a press statement. For example, a quote from a company chairman about intended expansion in overseas countries in a press release about the company's twenty-fifth anniversary.

These distinctions remain, such public relations people would probably agree, whether the press release or the press statement is sent by carrier pigeon, the post or the Internet.

If you prefer a hands-on approach to excessive reliance on electronics, remember that events such as conferences, even if they are not organized by you, can be an opportunity for you to convey your message, whatever it may be. If you attend any sort of industry, trade, professional or political conference, you may be able to put across to participants, as well as to journalists covering the conference, a story that benefits you or your organization. Go to all such events well prepared, if you or your organization has something to say.

But, in all circumstances, watch not only who you are speaking to but also those in whose *presence* you are speaking. If you are going to a radio or television studio to be questioned by a journalist as distinct from meeting a newspaper or magazine on your own home ground, ask at an early stage who else will be taking part in the programme – and follow up the point later if you cannot get a definite answer and are at all uneasy. In particular, is the studio to be packed with your worst enemies? If it is, you have the option of declining to take part or preparing tactics for defusing the opposition. Some people function better if under attack – it sharpens their wits most effectively. Others function worse. It is a question of personal temperament and professional practice.

Even if they are not hostile, the identity of other people taking part may condition how well you can get your points across. Suppose, on the publication of your first novel, you are invited to a radio studio to discuss it and the status and future of the novel generally. You ask who will be on the same programme and are told that an established novelist will be there. It is just as well to know that. You run the risk of being ignored in favour of the better-known voice, even though it is your novel that is supposed to be talked about.

In such a case, you might choose to prepare a series of verbal hand grenades with which to disrupt the flow if it is not running sufficiently in your favour. You will certainly have in your mind some arresting defence of your novel, and be prepared to advance it, unasked, if time is wasting away and your observations have not yet been sought.

On the other hand, it may be that one of the other people in the studio is someone it would pay you to court. Knowing in advance that he or she will be present will enable you to plan your charm offensive in advance.

The essence of media contact remains what it always has been: contact between people, not words on a screen, and certainly not unsourced words on a screen. Even if some sections of the electronic media appear to have cracked all the rules by giving fantasists and other time-wasters a very free rein, this may well not continue as these media become even more sophisticated and accountable.

At all events, they do not alter these central facts about contact with the media:

If, in the last analysis, you could not tell the truth about your motives and your actions, you have a substantial and possibly deserved problem.

But if in the last analysis, you could tell the truth, you may well in the shorter term feel that you are entitled to ration the truth as uttered by you to what presents you in the best possible light.

Avoiding telling lies to the media does not necessarily mean that you have a moral duty to act as your own prosecutor, unless you can do this as a rhetorical and preemptive way to rebut the prosecution case. But it does mean that, in case you are pressed, you should always have up your sleeve sound explanations for what you have done or intend to do.